JACQUES MARITAIN, like many another Catholic writer today, is a convert. While attending the Sorbonne around the turn of the century, he met his future wife Raïssa, and together they made the journey from *fin de siècle* rationalism to the Church.

At the suggestion of Charles Péguy, they began attending the lectures of Henri Bergson. From him they gained an insight into the inadequacy of positivism, though in other respects Bergsonian intuitionism failed to satisfy them. But soon after their marriage in 1904 they met the dynamic Leon Bloy, who probably had the deepest influence on their thought and ultimately led them to Catholicism.

Since then Maritain has lived the life of a scholar, teaching, writing, lecturing—and becoming the world's most famous Catholic philosopher. He received a tribute rare to one in his walk of life when the French Government named him ambassador to the Vatican in 1945. In recent years he has been attached to Princeton University, where he is now Professor Emeritus.

The range of Maritain's thought is seen in the subjects he has written about; logic, ethics, the philosophy of science, epistemology, aesthetics, mysticism, political philosophy, and metaphysics. A selection of his more important works includes *Art and Scholasticism, True Humanism; Science and Wisdom; The Degrees of Knowledge; Man and the State, Creative Intuition in Art and Poetry* and *An Introduction to Philosophy.*

The present volume, described by *Commonweal* as "profound and exhaustive," has already taken its place among his major works—and among the major writings on the vital problem of existentialism.

EXISTENCE
AND THE
EXISTENT

Jacques Maritain

English Version by
Lewis Galantiere and
Gerald B. Phelan

IMAGE BOOKS

A Division of
Doubleday & Company, Inc.
Garden City, New York

Image Books edition 1956
by special arrangement with Pantheon Books, Inc.

PRINTING HISTORY

Pantheon Books, Inc. edition published November 1948
1st printing . . . . November 1948
2nd printing . . . . July 1949

Image Books edition published February 1957
1st printing . . . . January 1957

Original French title:
Court Traité de l'Existence et de l'Existant

COVER BY RONALD CLYNE

TYPOGRAPHY BY EDWARD GOREY

To Raïssa

CONTENTS

EXISTENCE AND THE EXISTENT

INTRODUCTION

Varieties of "Existentialisms"

1. This brief treatise on existence and the existent may be described as an essay on the existentialism of St. Thomas Aquinas. It is important to obviate from the beginning any risk of confusion on this point. The 'existentialism' of St. Thomas is utterly different from that of the 'existentialist' philosophies propounded nowadays. If I say that it is, in my opinion, the only authentic existentialism, the reason is not that I am concerned to 'rejuvenate' Thomism, so to speak, with the aid of a verbal artifice which I should be ashamed to employ, by attempting to trick out Thomas Aquinas in a costume fashionable to our day. (The word 'costume,' in this connection, would certainly be a euphemism.) I am not a neo-Thomist. All in all, I would rather be a paleo-Thomist than a neo-Thomist. I am, or at least I hope I am, a Thomist. For more than thirty years I have remarked how difficult it is to persuade our contemporaries not to confuse the philosopher's faculty of invention with the ingenuity that inspires the art of the dress designer.

A Thomist who speaks of St. Thomas's existential-

ism is merely reclaiming his own, recapturing from
present-day fashion an article whose worth that
fashion itself is unaware of; he is asserting a prior
right. I shall add, for the sake of greater precision,
that in my view, what distinguishes authentic Thomism from the many non-Thomist, or allegedly Thomist currents in Scholasticism, into which the spirit
of Plato, Descartes, or Wolff has insinuated itself (a
spirit of which the so-called Thomism taught to-day
has not yet been completely purged), is precisely
the primacy which authentic Thomism accords to
existence and to the intuition of existential being. It
would be an excellent thing if, as a result of the stim-
ulus given by the contemporary systems of existentialism, attention was unmistakably directed to this
point. Even before these systems appeared, I had
already repeatedly pointed out the error of conceiving the philosophy of *being* as a philosophy of *essences* or as a dialectic of essences (what I call
thumbing through a picture-book) instead of seeing
that philosophy for what it really is, what constitutes
its peculiar advantage over all other philosophies
and gives it its unique and eminent place among
them, namely, the fact that it is the philosophy of
existence and of existential realism, the confronta-
tion of the act of existing by an intelligence determined never to disown itself.

As to vocabulary, it is commonly known that it is
chiefly owing to the influence of Kierkegaard that
the word 'existential' has become part of current
speech, particularly in Germany. Twenty years ago
there was a good deal of talk about existential Christianity, and I remember an eloquent lecture in which
Romano Guardini explained to a number of slightly
bewildered prelates that the existential meaning of

the Gospel of St. John had been revealed to him by the character of Prince Muyshkin in Dostoevski's *Idiot.* Many philosophers, from Jaspers and Gabriel Marcel to Berdyaeff and Chestov, were already calling themselves 'existential' philosophers. It was some time later that the word 'existentialism' passed into common usage, and with such success indeed that to-day, as M. Sartre remarked recently, 'it no longer signifies anything at all.' Apart from this incidental disadvantage, it is in itself a useful, nay an excellent word. As regards Thomist philosophy, it has this in common with the word realism, that it is not to be found in Peter of Bergamo's index. St. Thomas never proclaimed himself either an existentialist or a realist—though for that matter he never said he was a Thomist. The fact remains however that these things are consubstantial with his thought.

2. Let it be said right off that there are two fundamentally different ways of interpreting the word existentialism. One way is to affirm the primacy of existence, but as implying and preserving essences or natures and as manifesting the supreme victory of the intellect and of intelligibility. This is what I consider to be authentic existentialism. The other way is to affirm the primacy of existence, but as destroying or abolishing essences or natures and as manifesting the supreme defeat of the intellect and of intelligibility. This is what I consider to be apocryphal existentialism, the current kind which 'no longer signifies anything at all.' I should think so! For if you abolish essence, or that which *esse* posits, by that very act you abolish existence, or *esse.* Those two notions are correlative and inseparable. An existentialism of this sort is self-destroying.

However rationalistic he may have been, Descartes, in so far as he stemmed from Duns Scotus and was therefore the ancestor of the modern *libertistic* metaphysical systems, inclined towards this sort of existentialism in his view of God. It is quite true that he spoke endlessly of the divine essence, to the point of perceiving in it a kind of efficient cause of the very existence of God. But that essence became so absolutely impenetrable—except in so far as the idea of it was by itself sufficient to assure us of God's existence—that it was, so to say, no more than the sudden splendour of the very existence of God conceived as a pure act of will. Driven to its conclusion, this would give us a divine Existence devoid of any *nature*. And as this notion is unthinkable, our thought glides on to the more or less ambiguous substitute provided by the idea of a pure Action, a pure Efficiency, or Liberty, higher than the whole order of intellect or intelligibility, positing itself without reason, by virtue of its power alone, and arbitrarily creating intelligibles and essences as well as the ideas which portray them in our minds.

This, in the last analysis, is why the God of Descartes is a will entirely free from every order of wisdom (a position which St. Thomas looked upon as blasphemy). This is why such a God excludes from his action every sort of finality, creates eternal verities in the guise of pure contingents, which are not dependent upon his immutable essence (the possible participations of which his intelligence would immutably perceive), but upon his mere will. This is why he would have been able to create mountains without valleys, square circles, and contradictions both of which were equally true. This is why the entire order of human morality is afflicted (with respect to him) with the same radical contingency and is dependent upon a pure decree devoid of reason, the just and the unjust being such only by the good pleasure of his sovereign existence and by the unmotivated choice according to which the divine subject decides to exercise his creative liberty.

It is this same form of existentialism—in which the primacy of existence is asserted, but paid for by the abolition of intelligible nature or essence—that we find again in the atheistic existentialism of to-day; wherefore the author of *L'Etre et le Néant* has more reasons than he realises to hark back to the philosopher of the *cogito*. But this time it is no longer a matter of the supreme Existence on which an absolutist theism hangs a rationalist vision of the world, a vision which is all the more imperious for the fact that it originates in the mere good pleasure of inaccessible Infinity. This time it is the finite existence of subjects devoid of essence whom a primordial atheistic option flings into the chaos of slimy and disaggregated appearances that make up a radically irrational world, and whom it summons to make or create, not of course their essence or their intelligible structure, since those do not exist, but images launched into time, projects which fail again and again to furnish them with something like a countenance. This they are to do by making a succession of absolute and irrevocable choices which involve them irretrievably in the face of ever-new given situations.

An existence without essence, a subject without essence; from the very beginning we dwell in the unthinkable. Thereupon—and this absence of *fair play* is in my view the blackest stain on the philosophy in question[1]—there is substituted for the original affirmation, for the frank affirmation that existence is devoid of essence or excludes essence, the more elaborate and ambiguous affirmation that existence (Heidegger *dixit*) precedes essence. I say ambiguous, because it could signify something true (namely that act precedes potency, that my essence owes to my existence its very presence in the world, and that it owes its intelligibility to Existence in pure act), whereas in reality it signifies something totally different (namely that existence actuates

---

[1] I am quite aware that the notion of essence, like every other notion contained in the lexicon of metaphysics, has been re-cast in an entirely phenomenological perspective. Precisely because of this, if we are to call things by their right names, we are obliged to say that in the phenomenological existentialism that originates with Heidegger there is a radical *bad faith* which consists in appropriating to itself all the notions that we owe to the great metaphysicians of being, and which possess meaning only for the realistic intellect whose quest is the extra-mental mystery that surrounds what is. Those notions were appropriated for the purpose of exploiting them in the universe of phenomenological thought, the universe of the 'appearance which *is* essence' (*L'Etre et le Néant*, p. 12), where, in reality, they cease to possess meaning, but where, since the aim is to remain a metaphysician, they will continue to be used and corrupted in such a way that they may endlessly yield antinatural meanings. This sort of transcendental embezzlement could not but end in a tainted metaphysical system: phenomenology, under its existentialist aspect, is no more than a scholasticism corrupted at its root. Incidentally, this is what constitutes its undeniable historic interest. The metaphysics of being and scholasticism, though it be only in this corrupt form, is back in the main stream of modern philosophy, or rather, it makes plain to modern philosophy that a certain cycle has been completed. We may henceforth look forward to the birth of a new cycle in philosophy, both for good and for ill; and this corrupt scholasticism may perhaps be manuring the soil for a new germination of authentic metaphysics, at least wherever the earth shall have been vigorously enough ploughed.

nothing, that I exist but I am nothing, that man exists but there is no human nature).

In the same way, the notion of 'project'[2] is an ambiguous substitute for the notion of essence or quiddity, and that of situation is an ambiguous substitute for the notion of an objective conditioning resulting from the causes and natures interacting in the world. And just as, in the recesses of Descartes' metaphysics, the notions of pure Action, pure Efficiency, or pure Liberty were substituted for the unthinkable notion of a God without a nature, so here, for the unthinkable notion of a subject without a nature there is substituted the notion of pure action or pure efficiency as the exercise of an option— of pure liberty, in short, itself ambiguous and collapsing from within; for although it seems to appeal to a sovereign free will, it really appeals only to pure spontaneity, which is inevitably suspected of being merely the sudden explosion of necessities hidden in the depths of that nature which was allegedly exorcised. It was perhaps to all this that one critic was alluding when, in that matchless language in which philosophy nowadays rejoices, he reproached M. Sartre's doctrine with being a resurrection of radical-socialism.*

Let it be said that this doctrine is far less removed

[2] 'I emerge alone and in anguish in the face of the unique and first project that constitutes my being' (*L'Etre et le Néant*, p. 77). 'When I constitute myself as comprehension of a possible as *my* possible, I am obliged to recognise its existence at the terminus of my project, and to grasp it as myself, yonder, waiting for me in the future, separated from me by nothingness' (*Ibid.*, p. 79).

* French radical-socialism refers to a political party, representative of bourgeois liberalism which is neither 'radical' nor 'socialist' in the English meaning of these terms.—Translator's Note.

than Sartre himself believes from those 'professors in France who towards 1880 sought to establish a lay ethics'[3] by abolishing God and falling back upon bourgeois respectability and the Kantian decalogue. For if the existentialist thinks that it is very embarrassing that God should not exist; if he declares—thus displaying evidence of metaphysical perspicacity—that there is no human nature because there is no God to conceive it, and that, God once abolished, nothing in the world is intelligible; nevertheless, his point of departure, and the aim of the shrewd energy that informs his whole undertaking, is to provide this nauseating human vibrio, which persists in increasing and multiplying, with the means to get along in a world without God, and to shift for itself under atheism. (Not, of course, by retaining bourgeois respectability as a standard, but by finding ways not to be—to adopt Sartre's moral categories—a 'rascal' and a 'rotter.' This is another and doubtless more economical way, perhaps, of justifying one's existence. Neither are these means provided by imitating Descartes' God in arbitrarily setting up standards of justice and injustice and establishing an objective measure of morality, since no such thing exists, but in attributing a moral value, and even a heroic value to any act whatsoever, provided the act was undertaken in entire liberty.)

Here we have the inviolable arcana, the initial decision and the hygienic bias of existentialism: Manage at all costs to make atheism livable. But what if by chance that could not be managed? What if by chance a man could not get along, or adapt himself? The question does not even arise. It is deliber-

---

[3] J. P. Sartre, *L'Existentialisme est un Humanisme*, p. 34.

ately suppressed and forbidden. M. Sartre is right in declaring himself firmly optimistic and in leaving the tragic sense to Christians—to Christians and to the great anti-Christians. No need even to mention Pascal; in existentialism there is nothing equal to the stature of a Nietzsche. This astounding renunciation of any measure of grandeur is probably the most original and most highly appreciated contribution that existentialism has made to our age.

Chapter One

BEING

Veritas sequitur esse rerum

3. Thomas Aquinas, I have remarked in another essay,[1] reaches existence itself through the operation of the intellect itself. He has the most exactingly classical idea of science; he is scrupulously attentive to the slightest requirements and the most highly refined rules and measures of logic, of reason, and of the art of putting ideas together. What he knows is no picture-book, but is that very heaven and earth in which there are more things than are dreamt of in all the philosophies. It is that existent universe, set firmly upon primary facts, which we are required to discover, not deduce; that universe traversed by all the influxes productive of being which vivify it, unify it, cause it to push onward towards the unforeseeable future; that universe, also, which is wounded by all those deficiencies of being that constitute the reality of evil and in which we must see the price paid for the interaction of beings, the price paid for created liberty, capable of evading the influx of the First Being.

[1] J. Maritain, *De Bergson à Thomas d'Aquin*, Paris, 1927, p. 308.

Veritas sequitur esse rerum is the first Thomist position of which, in the present connection, we must note the significance. Truth follows upon the existence of things, i.e., of those trans-objective subjects with which thought stands face to face. Truth is the adequation of the immanence in act of our thought with that which exists outside our thought. True knowledge consists in a spiritual super-existence by which, in a supreme vital act, I become the other as such, and which corresponds to the existence exercised or possessed by that other itself in the particular field of intelligibility which is its peculiar possession.

Thus knowledge is immersed in existence. Existence—the existence of material realities—is given us at first by sense; sense attains the object as existing; that is to say, in the real and existing influence by which it acts upon our sensorial organs. This is why the pattern of all true knowledge is the intuition of the thing that I see, and that sheds its light upon me.[2] Sense attains existence in act without itself knowing that it is existence. Sense delivers existence to the intellect; it gives the intellect an intelligible treasure which sense does not know to be intelligible, and which the intellect, for its part, knows and calls by its name, which is *being*.

The intellect, laying hold of the intelligibles, disengaging them by its own strength from sense experience, reaches, at the heart of its own inner vitality, those natures or essences which, by abstracting them, it has detached from their material existence at a given point in space and time. But to what end? Merely in order to contemplate the picture of the

[2] Cf. Aristotle, *On the Heavens*, Bk. III; St. Thomas Aquinas, *De Veritate*, 12, 3, *ad* 2, and *ad* 3.

essences in its ideas? Certainly not! Rather in order to restore them to existence by the act in which intellection is completed and consummated, I mean the judgment pronounced in the words *ita est*, thus it is. When, for example, I say: 'In every Euclidean triangle the sum of the angles is equal to two right angles,' or, 'The earth revolves round the sun,' what I am really saying is that every Euclidean triangle *exists* in mathematical existence as possessing the property described; that the earth *exists* in physical existence as characterised by the movement described. The function of judgment is an existential function.[3]

Simple Apprehension

4. Some explanation is necessary concerning, in the first place, the abstractive perception which is the first operation of the mind, and, in the second place, judgment. On the first point we shall remark that a kind of holy horror comes over the existentialist philosophers, whether Christian or atheist, in the presence of what they call the universe of objects—a horror which, while on the one hand it entails serious results, to wit, the formal rejection of the conditions of intelligibility of knowledge, is, on the other

[3] J. Maritain, *De Bergson à Thomas d'Aquin*, pp. 309-311. When phenomenology elected gratuitously to recast concepts according to its method, the result, as concerns the existentialist phenomenologists, was to void the infinitive *to exist* of its natural content. As M. Michel Sora has rightly observed (*Du dialogue intérieur*, Paris, 1947, p. 30), *ex-sistere* does not mean 'to stand outside oneself' but 'to stand outside of one's causes,' or 'outside nothingness,' to emerge from the night of non-being, or from that of mere possibility, or that of potency.

hand, futile in origin, born as it is of a really shabby misunderstanding that goes far back in time to the Cartesian theory of idea-pictures.[4] They imagine, or construe the object as a reified idea, as a bit of pure externality, passive and inert, an obstacle to the mind, something interposing itself between the mind and the world of existence, or real subjects. Consequently, they contend that only the actual experience of subjectivity could reach those subjects. They do not see that object and objectivity are the very life and salvation of the intellect. The object is the term of the first operation of the intellect (simple perception, or 'simple apprehension'); what is it therefore if not, under a given specific aspect determined and cut out by abstraction, the intelligible density of an existent subject, rendered transparent in act to the mind and identified with the mind's vital activity by and in the concept? Briefly, the object as present in the mind is the intelligible objectisation of a trans-objective subject. But this trans-objective subject is, in its concrete existence, inexhaustible; therefore it admits of being attained in an indefinite number of new objects of concept linked to the preceding ones. Besides they do not see that this universe of objects which they seek industriously to drive out of existence does not in fact claim to exist in itself; it exists only in the mind; what exists is subjects, or supposita, objectised, indeed, in the mind in order to become known, but

---

[4] On the Cartesian theory of idea-pictures see J. Maritain, *Le songe de Descartes*, Paris, 1932, pp. 153 ff., Eng. trans., N. Y., 1944, pp. 168 ff. I have never identified the Cartesian idea with a *sensible* image, as M. Wahl believes. He seriously misunderstands my statement on this point. (Jean Wahl, *Tableau de la philosophie française*, Paris, 1947, p. 228.)

posited for themselves in the world of concrete and contingent existence where nature and adventure go hand in hand. I shall come back later to the importance in Thomist philosophy of this notion of subject or suppositum. From another and merely logical point of view I wish only to remark here that for this philosophy (following a distinction too often neglected) what a science tends to know is a determinate *subject* in its existential inexhaustibility, whereas the *object* of that science consists, in rigorous terms, in the conclusions to which the science leads.

The Marxists, for their part, are faithful to the notion of objects; but, biased as they are by an inverted Hegelianism and a dialectical idealism transmuted into a philosophy of the real, they actually neglect the universe of existence, or of subjects, and attribute an existence, that in reality is nothing but an extraposition of the Idea, to a universe of reified objects and of natures which are mere contingent aspects of the immanence of becoming. They thus leave themselves open to the accusation which the existentialists level against the idealistic myth of the object.

We may therefore dismiss them both to argue it out among themselves, and conclude our first consideration by saying that what the intellect, in abstractive perception (which is the first phase and condition of all its activity) lays hold of is not those eternal things which it would contemplate in some fanciful separate and intelligible universe, or mirage of hypostasised grammatical forms, proceeding from the shoddy Platonism which positivists and nominalists, existentialists and Marxists, consider inseparable from the notion of essences or natures endowed with unchangeable, intelligible structures. The metaphysician knows that his task is to search for the ultimate foundation of the intelligibility of things as of every other quality or perfection of being. He finds it in the pure Act, and understands that in the final analysis there would be no human nature if the divine Intellect did not perceive its own Essence, and in that Essence the eternal idea of man, which is not an abstract and universal idea, as our ideas are, but a creative idea. What we perceive, however, is not this divine idea; it is not in this intelligible heaven that we grasp human nature. The intelligible heaven in which we grasp and manipulate essences and natures is within ourselves, it is the active immanence of our immaterial thought. In that path which the intellect cuts through reality and sense experience in order to obtain its sustenance, that is to say, in abstractive perception, what the intellect lays hold of is the natures or essences which are in existent things or subjects (but not in the state of universality or intelligibility in act), which themselves are not things, and which the intellect strips of existence by immaterialising them. These are what, from the very beginning, we call intelligibles, or objects of thought.

Judgment

5. The second consideration, however, which concerns judgment, is what is chiefly important to us here. I said a moment ago that the function of judgment was an existential function, and that judgment restored the essences (the intelligibles, the objects of thought) to existence or to the world of subjects—to an existence that is either necessarily material, or

merely ideal, or (at least possibly) immaterial, accordingly as we deal with physical, mathematical, or metaphysical knowledge. Here a central problem arises, the problem of the philosophical significance of judgment, and of that existence itself which, according to Thomists, it is its function to affirm.

Descartes holds that judgment is an operation of the will, not of the intellect, and that the existence which it affirms is merely the positing of the *ideatum*, in itself inaccessible, of which the *idea* is the portrait. For Kant, judgment itself possesses an ideal and nonexistential function; it effects the concept by subsuming an empirical matter under a category; and existence is a mere positing absolutely devoid of all intelligible value or content. In St. Thomas's view, in contrast to that of Descartes, judgment is not only an operation which takes place following simple apprehension and the formation of the concept; it is the completion, the consummation, the perfection, and the glory of the intellect and of intellection, just as the existence it affirms is the glory and perfection of being and of intelligibility.

As I wrote in *The Degrees of Knowledge*,[5] when I 'form a judgment,' I accomplish on my *noemata*, within my thought, an operation which has meaning only because it relates to the fashion in which they exist (at least possibly) outside my thought. The function proper to judgment thus consists in transposing the mind from the plane of simple essence, of the simple *object* presented to thought, to the plane of the *thing*, of the subject possessing existence (actually or possibly) and of which the predicate-object of thought and the subject-object of thought are in-

---

[5] J. Maritain, *Les Degrés du savoir*, fourth ed., Paris, 1946, pp. 188-190. Eng. trans., London, 1937, pp. 117-119.

telligible aspects. In a different sense to Lask's, we may say with him that every judgment supposes an 'intact harmony' (on the side of the thing) and a 'reconciliation after struggle' (effected by the judgment itself). The 'embrace,' preceding that 'state of severance' which it is the function of judgment to 'vanquish,' is given in the thing, in the trans-objective subject. Judgment restores to the trans-objective subject its unity which simple apprehension (laying hold upon different objects of thought within that subject) had severed. This unity could not precede severance in the mind since the mind operates the other way round, dissolves the unity in order, subsequently, to re-establish it. In existence, outside the mind, this unity precedes severance (that is, is posited initially); and existence itself, inasmuch as it is something *had* (*exercita*), lies outside the order of simple representation or simple apprehension.

What does this mean? 'Judgment is not content with the representation or apprehension of existence. It affirms existence, it projects into it, as effected or effectible outside the mind, the objects of concept apprehended by the mind. In other words, when the intellect judges, it lives intentionally, by an act proper to itself, this same act of existing which the thing exercises or is able to exercise outside the mind.'[6] Existence thus affirmed and intentionally experienced by and in the mind is the consummation or completion, in the mind, of intelligibility in act. It corresponds to the act of existing exercised by things. And this act of existing is itself incomparably more than a mere positing without intelligible value of its own; it is act or energy *par excellence*; and

---

[6] *Les Degrés du savoir*, p. 191, note. Eng. trans., p. 119.

as we know, the more act there is the greater the intelligibility.

And yet existence is not an essence. It belongs to another order, an order which is other than the whole order of essences. It is therefore not an intelligible nor an object of thought in the sense given above to these words (which is synonymous with essence). What are we to conclude if not that existence goes beyond the object strictly so called, beyond the intelligible strictly so called, because it is an act exercised by a subject, whose eminent intelligibility, we may say super-intelligibility, objectises itself in us in the very act of judgment? In this sense we could call it a trans-objective act. It is in a higher and analogical sense that it is an intelligible. The intelligibility with which judgment deals is more mysterious than that which notions or ideas convey to us; it is not expressed in a concept but in the very act of affirming or denying. It is the super-intelligibility, if I may put it so, of the act of existing itself, either possible or actually given. And it is on this super-intelligibility of existence that St. Thomas hangs the whole life of the intellect.'[7]

✻

The Intuition of Being

6. This is why, at the root of metaphysical knowledge, St. Thomas places the intellectual intuition of that mysterious reality disguised under the most commonplace and commonly used word in the language, the word *to be;* a reality revealed to us as the

---

[7] J. Maritain, *De Bergson à Thomas d'Aquin,* p. 311.

uncircumscribable subject of a science which the gods begrudge us when we release, in the values that appertain to it, the act of existing which is exercised by the humblest thing—that victorious thrust by which it triumphs over nothingness.

A philosopher is not a philosopher if he is not a metaphysician. And it is the intuition of being—even when it is distorted by the error of a system, as in Plato or Spinoza—that makes the metaphysician. I mean the intuition of being in its pure and all-pervasive properties, in its typical and primordial intelligible density; the intuition of being *secundum quod est ens*.[8] Being, seen in this light, is neither the *vague* being of common sense, nor the *particularised* being of the sciences and of the philosophy of nature, nor the *de-realised* being of logic, nor the *pseudo*-being of dialectics mistaken for philosophy.[9] It is being disengaged for its own sake, in the values and resources appertaining to its own intelligibility and reality; which is to say, in that richness, that analogical and transcendental amplitude which is *inviscerated* in the imperfect and multiple unity of its concept and which allows it to cover the infinitude of its analogates and causes it to overflow or superabound in transcendental values and in dynamic values of propensity through which the idea of being transgresses itself.[10] It is being, attained or perceived at the summit of an abstractive intellection, of an eidetic or intensive visualisation which

[8] St. Thomas, *In Metaph. Arist.*, IV, 1, (Cathala ed., pp. 530-533).

[9] Cf. J. Maritain, *Sept Leçons sur l'Etre*, Paris, n.d., pp. 35-50, Eng. trans., *A Preface to Metaphysics*, N. Y., 1939, pp. 33-42.

[10] Ibid., *Leçons* iii and iv, Eng. trans., pp. 43-89.

owes its purity and power of illumination only to the fact that the intellect, one day, was stirred to its depths and trans-illuminated by the impact of the act of existing apprehended in things, and because it was quickened to the point of receiving this act, or hearkening to it, within itself, in the intelligible and super-intelligible integrity of the tone peculiar to it.

There are diverse ways and paths leading towards the attainment of this intuition. None is traced in advance, none is more legitimate than another—precisely because here there is no question of rational analysis or of an inductive or a deductive procedure, or of a syllogistic construction, but only of an intuition which is a primary fact. The senses, and what St. Thomas calls the 'judgment of sense,' the blind existential perception exercised by the senses, play here a primordial and indispensable part. But this is no more than a prerequisite; the eyes of him who was blind from birth must be opened; the touch of the spiritual virtues of the intellect must release into intelligible light this act of existing which sense attains without discovering it and touches without perceiving it. It matters little whether the intuition of being resemble the innate gift of an imperial intelligence serenely relying upon its limpid strength and upon the cooperation of a pure and delicate flesh, and of a vivid and perfectly balanced sensibility, as seems to have been the case for Thomas Aquinas; whether, alternatively, it spring unexpectedly like a kind of natural grace at the sight of a blade of grass or a windmill, or at the sudden perception of the reality of the self; whether it proceed from the implacability with which the being of things independent of ourselves becomes abruptly evident to us, suddenly casting our own being back upon its solitude and its frailty; whether I make my way towards it by inner experience of duration, or of anguish, or of certain moral realities which transcend the flow of time—these alternatives, I repeat, are of slight moment. What counts is to take the leap, to release, in one authentic intellectual intuition, the sense of being, the sense of the value of the implications that lie in the act of existing. What counts is to have seen that existence is not a simple empirical fact but a primitive datum for the mind itself, opening to the mind an infinite supra-observable field—in a word, the primary and super-intelligible source of intelligibility.

It is not enough to teach philosophy, even Thomist philosophy, in order to possess this intuition. Let us call it a matter of luck, a boon, perhaps a kind of docility to the light. Without it man will always have an opining, precarious and sterile knowledge, however freighted with erudition it may be; a *knowledge about*. He will go round and round the flame without ever going through it. With it, even though he stray from the path, he will always go farther than he can advance by years of mere dialectical exercise, critical reflection, or conceptual dissection of phenomena; and he will have the added privilege of solitude and melancholy. If the poet can be called a seer, the philosopher is no less entitled to this name, though in his own way. He may at times be the victim of some bewilderment; but at other times he will know the joy of discovery; and for all of the knowledge he will have got out of books, for all of his knowledge of life, he will owe both bewilderment and joy to the fact that he remains enraptured with being.

The Concept of Existence or of To-exist (esse)
and that of Being or of That-which is (ens)

7. The foregoing reflections face us with a paradox which we must attempt to clear up. We said
that the intelligible apprehended in our ideas was
essence. But existence is not an essence; it is shut off
from the whole order of essence. How then can it be
the object of the intellect, and its supreme object?
How can we speak of the concept or the idea of existence? Ought we not to say rather that existence is
not apprehended by the intellect, or apprehensible
by it? that existence does not admit of conceptualisa-
tion, is no more than a limit (set up on every side
by reality) upon the philosophical chase after essences? that existence is an unknowable upon which
metaphysics builds without itself attaining to it?

What has already been said gives a premonition
of the answer. Essences are the object of the first
operation of the intellect, or *simple apprehension.*
It is *judgment* which the act of existing confronts.
The intellect envelops itself and is self-contained,
is wholly present in each of its operations; and in
the initial upsurge of its activity out of the world of
sense, in the first act of self-affirmation accomplished
by expressing to itself any datum of experience, it
apprehends and judges in the same instant. It forms
its first idea (that of being) while uttering its first
judgment (of existence), and utters its first judgment while forming its first idea. I say, therefore,
that it thus lays hold of the treasure which properly
belongs to judgment, in order to envelop it in simple
apprehension itself; it visualises that treasure in an

initial and absolutely original idea, in a privileged idea which is not the result of the process of simple apprehension alone, but of the laying hold of that which the intellect affirms from the moment it judges, namely, the act of existing. It seizes upon the eminent intelligibility or the super-intelligibility which the act of judging deals with (that of existence), in order to make of it an object of thought.

Thus existence is made object; but, as I pointed out earlier, in a higher and analogical sense resulting from the objectising of a trans-objective act and referring to trans-objective subjects that exercise or are able to exercise this act. Here a concept seizes upon that which is not an essence but is an intelligible in a higher and analogical sense, a super-intelligible delivered up to the mind in the very operation which it performs each time that it judges, and from the moment of its first judgment.

But this concept of existence, of *to-exist* (*esse*) is not and cannot be *cut off* from the absolutely primary concept of being (*ens*, that-which is, that-which exists, that whose act is to exist). This is so because the affirmation of existence, or the judgment, which provides the content of such a concept, is itself the 'composition' of a subject with existence, i.e., the affirmation that *something exists* (actually or possibly, simply or with such-and-such a predicate). It is the concept of being (that-which exists or is able to exist) which, in the order of ideative perception, corresponds adequately to this affirmation in the order of judgment. The concept of existence cannot be visualised completely apart, detached, isolated, separated from that of being; and it is in that concept of being and with that concept of being that it is at first conceived. Here we touch upon the original error that underlies all the modern existentialist philosophies. Ignorant of or neglecting the warning of the old scholastic wisdom, that 'the *act of existing* cannot be the object of a perfect abstraction,' these philosophies presuppose that existence can be isolated. They contend that existence alone is the nourishing soil of philosophy. They treat of existence without treating of being.[11] They call themselves philosophies of existence instead of calling themselves philosophies of being.

All this simply amounts to saying that the concept of existence cannot be detached from the concept of essence. Inseparable from each other, these two make up one and the same concept, simple although intrinsically varied; one and the same essentially analogous concept, that of being. This is the first of all concepts, because it springs in the mind at the first awakening of thought, at the first intelligible coming to grips with the experience of sense by transcending sense. All other concepts are variants or determinations of this primary one. At the instant when the finger points to that which the eye sees, at the instant when sense perceives, in its blind fashion, without intellection or mental word, that *this exists;* at that instant the intellect says (in a judgment), *this being is* or *exists* and at the same time (in a concept), *being.*[12] We have here a mutual in-

---

[11] Or rather (and this is no better) they claim, as Heidegger does, to propound a treatise on being when, starting from existence or rather from the existential spot of actuality, they only phenomenalise it.

[12] Of course, I am not speaking here of verbally formulated operations, nor even of operations explicitly thought. The essential thing is that they be there implicitly, *in actu exercito.* There are primitive languages which do not possess the word 'being.' But the idea of being is implicitly

volution of causes, a reciprocal priority of this concept and this judgment, each preceding the other in a different order. To say, 'this being is or exists,' the idea of being must be present. To have the idea of being, the act of existing must have been affirmed and grasped in a judgment. Generally speaking, simple apprehension precedes judgment in the later stages of the process of thinking; but here, at the first awakening of thought, each depends upon the other. The idea of being ('this being') precedes the judgment of existence in the order of material or subjective causality; and the judgment of existence precedes the idea of being in the order of formal causality. The more one ponders this issue, the more it appears that this is how the intellect conceptualises existence and forms its idea of being—of the *vague* being known to common sense.

8. When, moving on to the queen-science, metaphysics, and to that higher intuition of which I spoke a while back, the intellect disengages being from the knowledge of the sensible in which it is immersed, in order to make it the object or rather the subject of metaphysics; when, in a word, it conceptualises the metaphysical intuition of being (seen now in the light of all the values proper to it, in its typical and primordial intelligible density), what the intellect releases into that same light[13] is, here again, first and foremost, the act of existing.

---

present in the mind of the primitive men who use those languages. The first idea formed by a child is not the idea of being; but the idea of being is implicit in the first idea which the child forms.

[13] At the moment when sense apprehends an existent sensible, the concept of being and the judgment, 'this being exists,' which condition each other, arise simultaneously in

At that point, according to classical Thomist doc-

the intellect, as I have pointed out above. In this first of
all our concepts released for its own sake, the metaphysical
intellect perceives being in its analogical amplitude and in
its freedom with respect to empirical conditions. With this
notion as point of departure—a notion whose fecundity is
inexhaustible—metaphysics formulates the first divisions of
being and the first principles. The principle of identity has
a significance which is not only 'essential' or 'copulative'
('every being is what it is'), but also and primarily existential ('that which exists, exists'). (Cf. Sept Leçons sur
l'Etre, p. 105, Eng. trans., pp. 93-94.) When, by the 'reflection' which judgment has primed, the subject grasps
itself as existent, and grasps the extra-mental existence of
things, it merely renders reflexively explicit that which it
already knew. The extra-mental existence of things was
given to it from the very start in the intuition and concept
of being. (I mean to say that this intuition presents being
according to the very analogicity of this concept, so that
being is grasped as existing, actually or possibly, contingently or necessarily; and that, in the particular analogate
of being most immediately attained—the sensible existent,
and, more generally speaking, things—this extra-mental
existence is given as contingent and not as forming part of
the notion of things.)

In other words, the following stages should be distinguished:

1. 'Judgment' (improperly so-called) of the external
senses and the aestimative, such as it is found in animals,
and bearing upon a sensible existent given to perception.
This is, in the sphere of sense (with its treasure of intelligibility in potency, but in no wise in act) the 'blind' equivalent of what we express in saying, 'this exists.'

2. Formation—in one simultaneous awakening of the intellect and the judgment which mutually involve each
other—of an idea ('this being' or simply 'this thing' in which
the idea of being is implicitly present) and a judgment
composing the object of thought in question with the act of
existing (not with the notion of existence, but with the act
of existing): 'this thing exists' or 'this being exists.'

In forming this judgment the intellect, on the one hand,
knows the subject as singular (indirectly and by 'reflection
upon phantasms'), and, on the other hand, affirms that this
singular subject exercises the act of existing. In other words,
the intellect itself exercises upon the notion of this subject

trine, it has reached the third degree of abstraction.[14] But it is clear from this how false it would

---

an act (the act of affirming) by which it lives intentionally
the existence of the thing. This affirmation has the same
content as the 'judgment' of the aestimative and the external sense (but in this case that content is no longer 'blind'
but openly revealed since it is raised to the state of intelligibility in act); and it is not by reflection upon phantasms
that the intellect proffers the affirmation, but by and in
this 'judgment' itself, and in this intuition of sense which
it grasps by immaterialising it, in order to express it to
itself. It thus reaches the *actus essendi* (in judging)—as it
reaches essence (in conceiving)—*by the mediation of sensorial perception*.

3. Formation of the idea of existence.—From the point
when, conjointly with the first judgment of existence, the
idea of being ('that which exists or is able to exist') has
thus emerged, the intellect grasps the *act* of existing affirmed
in the first judgment of existence, in order to make of it
an *object* of thought; it makes unto itself a concept or notion of existence (*existentia ut significata*).

4. Intuition of first principles, especially of the principle
of identity ('that which exists, exists'; 'every being is what
it is').

5. Only thereafter, by an *explicit* reflection upon its act,
does the intellect become explicitly conscious of the existence of the thinking subject. It does not merely live the
cogito, it expresses it. And by opposition:

6. It knows explicitly, as extra-mental, the being and the
existence which in their extra-mental reality had already
been given to it in fact at stages 2, 3, and 4.

This analysis concurs with that of Father Garrigou-
Lagrange (De intelligentia naturali et de primo objecto ab
ipsa cognito, in *Acta Pontif. Acad. Romanae S. Thoma Aq.*,
Rome, 1940) in that it places the intuition of the principle
of identity *before* the moment when the thinking subject
becomes conscious of its own existence. It differs in placing the first judgment of existence (which conditions the
formation of the idea of being and is conditioned by it)
before the moment when the thinking subject becomes conscious of its own existence and even *before* the intuition of
the principle of identity.

[14] The doctrine expounded by St. Thomas in the commentary on the *De Trinitate* of Boethius (in *De Trin.*, q. 5,

be to place the degrees of abstraction upon the same
line as if mathematics were merely more abstract

a. 3, c.; cf. the important note in which Father Geiger cites
the article in question in its exact import and from the
autographic manuscript: L. B. Geiger, *La Participation dans
la philosophie de saint Thomas d'Aquin*, Paris, 1942, pp.
318-319) confirms the thesis that the metaphysical concept
of being, as earlier the common sense concept formed by
the intellect upon its first awakening, is an eidetic visualisation of being apprehended in judgment, in the *secunda
operatio intellectus, quae respicit ipsum esse rei*. This doctrine shows indeed that what properly pertains to the metaphysical concept of being is that it results from an
abstraction (or a separation from matter) which takes place
secundum hanc secundam operationem intellectus. ('Hac
operatione intellectus vere abstrahere non potest, nisi ea quae
sunt secundum rem separata.') If it can be separated from
matter by the operation of the (negative) judgment, the
reason is that it is related in its content to the act of existing which is signified by the (positive) judgment and which
over-passes the line of material essences—the connatural
object of simple apprehension.

In this article on the *De Trinitate* St. Thomas reserves
the noun *abstractio* strictly understood for the operation by
which the intellect considers and grasps separately an object of thought which in reality cannot exist without the
other things which the intellect leaves outside its consideration. (Wherefore, 'ea quorum unum sine alio intelligitur
sunt simul secundum rem.') When, accordingly, he distinguishes between the *abstractio* 'common to all the sciences'
(first degree of intensive abstraction) and the *abstractio
formae a materia sensibili* which is proper to mathematics
(second degree of intensive abstraction) on the one hand,
and, on the other hand, the *separatio* proper to metaphysics
where, because it takes place *secundum illam operationem
quae componit et dividit,* the intellect divides one thing
from another *per hoc quod intelligit unum alii non inesse,*
he means (as he teaches constantly, for example, in his
commentary on the Metaphysics) that things which are the
object of metaphysics *exist or are able to exist without matter,* are or are able to be separated from every material
condition in the very existence they exercise outside the
mind (*separatio secundum ipsum esse rei*). It is in a judgment declaring that being is *not* necessarily linked to matter
nor to any of its conditions that the intellect abstracts being

and more general than physics, and metaphysics
more abstract and more general than mathematics.

from all matter and makes for itself the metaphysical concept of being as being. If St. Thomas thus emphasises the
distinction between the *separatio* proper to metaphysics and
the mere *abstractio* which belongs to the other sciences, the
reason is that he seeks to show, against the Platonists, that
transcendentals can exist apart from matter, but that universals and mathematicals cannot. 'Et quia quidam non
intellexerunt differentiam duorum ultimorum (common abstraction and mathematical abstraction) a primo (metaphysical 'separation'), inciderunt in errorem, ut ponerent mathe-
matica et universalia a sensibilibus separata, ut Pythagorici
et Platonici.'

There is nothing more to be looked for in these texts,
and they do not at all signify that the *separatio* in question
ought to be substituted for the 'abstraction called analogical'
(third degree of intensive abstraction). The fact that St.
Thomas here employs the word *separatio* rather than the
word *abstractio* (reserved for cases where the object separately grasped cannot exist separately) in no wise prevents
this *separatio*—since it ends in an idea, and an idea the
object signified by which is the farthest removed from matter—from being an abstraction in the general or rather pro-
portional meaning of the word (but which is not produced
in the line of simple apprehension of essences!). This
'separation' *is* the analogical abstraction of being.

In this very text St. Thomas, as a matter of fact, employs
the word *abstrahere* with reference to the separation which
takes place in judgment: 'Secundum hanc secundam operationem intellectus *abstrahere* non potest vere quod secundum
rem conjunctum est, quia in *abstrahendo* significatur esse
separatio secundum ipsum esse rei, sicut si *abstraho* homi-
nem ab albedine dicendo: homo non est albus, significo
separationem esse in re. . . . Hac igitur operatione intellectus vere *abstrahere* non potest, nisi ea quae sunt secundum
rem separata, ut cum dicitur: homo non est asinus.'

Between the *triplex distinctio* of the commentary on the
De Trinitate of Boethius and the three degrees of abstraction of Cajetan and John of St. Thomas there is a difference
of vocabulary, there is no difference of doctrine. The doctrine of the three degrees of abstraction has its basis in the
Metaphysics of Aristotle, where it finds an equivalent for-
mulation. Cf. St. Thomas, *In Metaph. Aristotelis* Prooemium, VI, 1, Cathala ed., 1156-1165; XI, 7, Cathala ed.,

By no means! What is common to the three degrees
of abstraction is only analogically common to them.
Each corresponds to a typically and irreducibly different manner of confronting and grasping reality,
to a 'hold' that is *sui generis* in the struggle of the
intellect with things. The abstraction proper to metaphysics does not proceed from a 'simple apprehension' or an eidetic visualisation of a universal more
universal than the others. It proceeds from the
eidetic visualisation of a transcendental which permeates everything and whose intelligibility involves
an irreducible proportionality or analogy—*a* is to its
own *act of existing* (*esse*) as *b* is to its own *act of
existing* (*esse*),—because this is precisely what judgment discovers, namely, the actuation of a being by
the act of existing, grasped as extending beyond
the limits and conditions of empirical existence;
grasped, therefore, in the limitless amplitude of its
intelligibility.

If metaphysics is established at the highest degree
of abstraction, the reason is precisely that, unlike all
the other sciences, in concerning itself with being as
being, as a proper object of analysis and scientific
disquisition, it concerns itself with the very act of
existing. The object of metaphysics is being, or that
whose act is to exist, considered in its quality as being, that is to say, according as it is not linked to the
material conditions of empirical existence, according
as it exercises or is able to exercise, without matter,
the act of existing. In virtue of the type of abstrac-

2259-2264. On this doctrine of degrees of abstraction cf.
my writings: *Les Degrés du savoir*, pp. 71-76, 265-268, 414-
432, Eng. trans., pp. 44-47, 165-167, 257-268; *Sept Leçons
sur l'Etre*, pp. 85-96; Eng. trans., pp. 75-86. *Quatre Essais
sur l'Esprit dans sa condition charnelle*, Paris, 1939, pp. 231-
232, 237-238.

tion which characterises it, metaphysics considers
realities which exist, or are able to exist, without
matter. It abstracts from the material conditions of
empirical existence, but it does not abstract from existence! Existence is the terms as a function of which
metaphysics knows everything that it does know; I
say, real existence, either actual or possible, not existence as a singular datum of sense or of consciousness, but as disengaged from the singular by abstractive intuition; existence not reduced to this moment
of existential actuality actually experienced (in
which alone the existentialist phenomenologists are
interested) but liberated in that intelligible amplitude which it possesses as the act of that which is,
and which affords a grasp on the necessary and universal certainties of a scientific knowledge properly
so-called. Moreover, it is in things themselves that
metaphysics finds its object. It is the being of sensible and material things, the being of the world of
experience, which is its immediately accessible field
of investigation;[15] it is this which, before seeking its
cause, it discerns and scrutinises—not as sensible and
material, but as being. Before rising to the level of
spiritual existents, it is empirical existence, the existence of material things, that it holds in its grasp

---

[15] The *goal* of metaphysics is knowledge of the *cause* of
being-common-to-the-ten-predicaments, but its *subject* is
that *common being* itself: 'Quamvis autem subjectum hujus
scientiae sit ens commune, dicitur tamen tota de his quae
sunt separata a material secundum esse et rationem. Quia
secundum esse et rationem separari dicuntur, non solum
illa quae nunquam in material esse possunt, sicut Deus et
intellectuales substantiae, sed etiam *illa quae possunt sine
materia esse, sicut ens commune*. Hoc tamen non contin-
geret, si a materia secundum esse dependerent.' St. Thomas
Aquinas, *In Metaph. Aristotelis*, Prooemium.

—though not as empirical and material, but as existence.

Thus, its being more universal than the other sciences is but a quasi-incidental consequence of the immateriality of its object and its vision. By the nature of metaphysical knowledge and by the very fact that its own peculiar insight (which consists in seeing that which, according to its proper intelligible constitutive characteristics, is free of matter) enables it to penetrate into things without being halted by material characteristics, metaphysics is concerned with that which is most profound in things concrete and individual—their being, discovered in its quality of being and in the act of existing which things exercise or are able to exercise. If it does not reach individuality, that is not because it cannot do so by reason of its own noetic structure. I should say that that is not its own fault; rather, it is the fault of matter, which is, in the individual, the root of non-being and unintelligibility. The proof of this is that when metaphysics passes from being to the cause of being, the supreme reality that it knows (wrapped, it is true, in the veils of analogy) is the supremely individual reality, the reality of the pure Act, the *Ipsum esse subsistens*. It is the only science that is able to reach the individual, I mean, the individual *par excellence*. The worst metaphysical heresy is that which regards being as the *genus generalissimum* and makes of it at one and the same time a univocal thing and a pure essence. Being is not a universal; its infinite amplitude, its super-universality, if the reader prefers, is that of an implicitly multiple object of thought which, analogically, permeates all things and descends, in its irreducible diversity, into the very heart of each: it is not merely that which they are, but is also their very act of existing.

There is a concept of existence. In this concept, existence is taken *ut significata*,[16] as signified to the mind after the fashion of an essence, although it is not an essence. But metaphysics does not treat of the concept of existence; no science stops at the concept; all sciences proceed through it to reality.[17] It is not of the concept of existence, it is of existence itself that the science of being treats. And when it treats of existence (it always treats of it, at least in some fashion) the concept of which it makes use does not display to it an essence but, as Etienne Gilson puts it,[18] that which has for its essence not to be an essence. There is analogy, not univocity, between such a concept and the concepts of which the other sciences make use. They use their concepts in order to know the realities signified by those concepts; but those realities are essences. Metaphysics uses the concept of existence in order to know a reality which is not an essence, but is the very act of existing.

I have mentioned that the concept of existence cannot be detached from that of essence: existence is always the existence of something, of a capacity to exist. The very notion of *essentia* signifies a relation to *esse*, which is why we have good grounds

[16] Cf. Cajetan, *In Sum. theol.*, 1, 2, 1, *ad* 2; and my *Songe de Descartes*, pp. 192-198, Eng. trans., pp. 131-132.

[17] Which holds also for faith: 'Actus credentis non terminatur ad enuntiabile, sed ad rem' holds also for science: 'Non enim formamus enuntiabilia nisi ut per ea de rebus cognitionem habeamus, sicut in scientia, ita et in fide.' St. Thomas, *Sum. theol.*, II-II, 1, 2, *ad* 2.

[18] Cf. Etienne Gilson, 'Limites existentielles de la philosophie,' in *L'Existence*, Paris, 1945, p. 80.

for saying that existence is the primary source of intelligibility.[19] But, not being an essence or an intelligible, this primary source of intelligibility has to be a super-intelligible. When we say that being is *that which exists or is able to exist, that which exercises or is able to exercise existence,* a great mystery is contained in these few words. In the subject, *that which,* we possess an essence or an intelligible—in so far as it is this or that, in so far as it possesses a nature. In the verb *exists* we have the act of existing, or a super-intelligible. To say *that which exists* is to join an intelligible to a super-intelligible; it is to have before our eyes an intelligible engaged in and perfected by a super-intelligibility. Why should it be astonishing that at the summit of all beings, at the point where everything is carried to pure transcendent act, the intelligibility of essence should fuse in an absolute identity with the super-intelligibility of existence, both infinitely overflowing what is designated here below by their concepts, in the incomprehensible unity of *Him Who is?*

*

The Implications of the Intuition of Being

9. I have tried to state precisely some aspects of the fundamental intuition upon which everything in Thomism depends. A commentary upon this intuition of being would be endless.[20] The most fundamental and most characteristic metaphysical thesis of Aristotelianism as re-thought by Thomas Aquinas,

[19] Cf. above, pp. 20, 21.

[20] Cf. J. Maritain, *Sept Leçons sur l'Etre, Leçons* iii to vi. Eng. trans., pp. 43 ff.

the thesis of the real distinction between essence
and existence in all that is not God—in other words,
the extension of the doctrine of potency and act to
the relation between essence and existence, is directly connected with this intuition. This is, in truth,
a thesis of extreme boldness, for in it potency (essence, or intelligible structure already achieved in
its own line of essence) is completed or actuated by
an act *of another order* which adds absolutely nothing to essence as essence, intelligible structure, or
quiddity, yet adds everything to it in as much as it
posits it *extra causas* or *extra nihil*. We can understand nothing of this if we confine ourselves within
a purely essentialist perspective, if we do not see
that the very intelligibility of the essences—I say, in
things, not in our mind, where they are separated
from things—if we do not see that the very intelligibility of essences is a certain kind of ability to
exist. *Potentia dicitur ad actum:* knowability or intelligibility, essence, is to be understood in its relationship to the act of existing. The analogical infinitude of the act of existing is a created participation
in the unflawed oneness of the infinity of the *Ipsum
esse subsistens;* an analogical infinitude which is diversified according to the *possibilities* of existing. In
relation to it those very possibilities of existing, the
essences, are knowable or intelligible. Made real by
the act of existing—that is to say, placed outside the
state of simple possibility—they are really distinct
from it as potency is really distinct from the act that
actuates it; for if they were their own existence they
would be Existence and Intelligibility in pure act,
and would no longer be created essences.

Thus the act of existing is the act *par excellence*.
Whether we consider it in this humble blade of grass

or in the feeble beating of our heart, it is everywhere
the act and the perfection of all form and all perfection. *Hoc quod dico esse est actualitas omnium
actuum, et propter hoc est perfectio omnium perfec-
tionum.*[21] 'The act of existing is the actuality of every form or nature';[22] 'it is the actuality of all things,
and even of forms themselves.'[23] The act of existing,
which is not an essence, which is neither this nor
that, and which could not be called act or energy or
form or perfection if these words were univocal and
could not designate something outside the whole order of essence, the act of existing is that which is
most actual and most formal, *illud quod est maxime
formale omnium est ipsum esse,*[24] *ipsum esse est
perfectissimum omnium.*[25] St. Thomas is fully convinced that a living dog is better than a dead lion[26]
—though he also thinks, to the annoyance of some,
that a lion (living) is better than a dog. And he is
convinced also that beyond the whole order of being, *extra omne genus respectu totius esse,*[27] 'God
contains within himself all the perfection of being'
because He is Being itself, or 'the very act of existing,
subsistent by itself.'[28] The first cause is above that
which is or that which has being (*supra ens*); not,
as the Platonists believed, because the essence of
goodness and of unity was higher than being conceived as a separate essence, but because the first

[21] St. Thomas, *De Pot.*, 7, 2, *ad* 9.
[22] *Sum. theol.*, I, 3, 4, c.
[23] *Ibid.*, I, 4, 1, *ad* 3.
[24] *Ibid.*, I, 7, 1, c.
[25] *Ibid.*, I, 4, 1, *ad* 3.
[26] *Ecclesiastes*, IX, 4.
[27] *Sum. theol.*, I, 3, 6, *ad* 2.
[28] *Sum. theol.*, I, 4, 2, c.

cause is the infinite act of existence itself, *inquantum est ipsum esse infinitum*.[29]

10. It could be easily shown that all the other great specifically Thomist theses also possess meaning only for a mind turned in the first instance towards existence. This is why they will always be disputed by every philosophy that is not centered upon the primacy of the act of existing.

It is thus with the theory of universals and with that of the virtual distinction. If universals are based upon things, yet are not to be found as such except in the mind; if there is no middle ground between real distinction and distinction of reason, the explanation is that the way in which things exercise the act of existing relegates to purely ideal existence all the conditions of existence which they don as objects of thought.

It is the same with the theory of potency and particularly that of *materia prima*. If potency is in no wise a rough sketch of act or a virtuality, the reason is that the world is not a dictionary of essences or of ideal possibles, each intelligible by itself, be it only as mere sketch or mere virtuality, but that there is in things a dimension of opacity or of radical unintelligibility—a deposit of reality not intelligible by itself—which lies the deeper in proportion to the distance which separates things from the pure act of existing. If matter is absolutely without act, form, or determination, the reason is that it is not an essence but merely a potency, even in relation to essence; and if it is not an essence the reason is that essence is to be understood in relation to the act of existing;

[29] *Comm. in Libr. de Causis, Lectio 6.*

and that which does not in itself constitute a possibility of existing is not an essence.

It is the same with the theory of the human composite. If the spiritual and subsistent soul is the unique and substantial form of the human substance, and if man is not made up of two juxtaposed essences (as Cartesian spiritualism would have it, to the misfortune of modern thought); if man is a single natural whole—biological, sentient, rational—in virtue of the actuation of *materia prima* by a form which is a spirit, the reason is that form (like essence) of itself implies a relationship to existence (*esse per se convenit formae*) and that it ought not to be conceived only as that by which a subject possesses in its essences such-and-such intelligible determinations, but also as that by which it is determinately constituted for existing and receives from its causes existential actuation. In an essentialist perspective, the intellective soul is only that by which I think; and extension (or any other material form) is that by which I have a body. But in an existentialist perspective the intellective soul is that by which existence takes hold of my whole self, my body and my senses and my thought as well, and is that by which the prime matter itself which it informs is maintained in existence.

It is the same with the theory of evil. If evil, though it be an absence or lack of being, is by no means a mere diminution of good; and if it is real and if it is active and if it even has enough power to undo the work of God, the reason is that it is not a mere lacuna in an essence but is a privation within a subject exercising the act of existing, a wound in existence; and further because, acting not by itself but by the good in which it 'nihilates,'* evil is the more active and the stronger as this existent subject which it wounds by non-being is the more deeply wounded and itself exercises a more active and a higher existence.

It is the same with the theory of the immanent acts of knowing and loving. No analysis conducted in terms of essence is capable of giving account of these acts. It is in terms of existence that they require to be conceived—at which moment each of them appears as a typical manner of actively super-existing: knowledge as the immaterial super-existence in which the knower intentionally is, or becomes, the known; love as the immaterial super-existence in which the beloved is or becomes, in the lover, the principle of a gravitational pull or intentional connaturality by which the lover tends inwardly towards existential union with the beloved, as towards its own being from which it has been separated, and thus loses itself in the reality of the beloved.[30]

It is the same with the theory of liberty regarded as an indetermination, not potential but active and dominating, and as the mastery of the will over the very judgment that determines it. There is here, in the last analysis, a primacy of exercise over specification which shocks every philosophy of pure essence

---

* The coinages 'nihilate' and 'nihilation' will be used throughout this translation to render the French words (also coined) *néanter* and *néantement*. 'To nihilate' does not mean 'to give non-being,' which would rather be expressed by the word 'negate,' nor does it mean 'to deprive of being' or 'annihilate.' It signifies simply *to abstain from giving being*.—Translator's Note.

[30] *Les Degrés du savoir*, pp. 734-736. Eng. trans., pp. 452-453.

and which has meaning only because at the indivisible instant when will and intellect determine each other, the act of the will causes the subject to exist, *decidedly,* according to the particular attitude or disposition of its whole moral nature, in relation to which a particular good will be appropriate to that subject; and that same act of the will renders the corresponding judgment of the intellect efficacious, or, in other words, causes it to get a grip on existence *decidedly.**

It is the same with the theory of divine motion in respect of human liberty. If the divine motion determined the human will in the way that, in the world of essences, coordinates determine a direction, or a perpendicular determines a point on a line, we should never be able to understand how the human will can remain free while it is being moved by God. But everything changes when the mind places itself in the perspective of the act of existing; and when we understand, on the contrary, that human liberty (that sovereign actuality which consists in the dominating indetermination and mastery of the will over the judgment which determines it) could not act, could not be exercised, if the motion of the first cause did not activate it from within to realise itself in existence, as it activates all causes according to their own mode of acting to the exercise of their existential act.

More generally, indeed, it is clear that the notions of efficient cause and of finality, which are so natural to common sense but so thorny for philosophers, and upon which all the great modern metaphysical

---

* 'Decidedly,' that is, consequent upon a decision, as to exist 'intentionally' is a mode consequent upon a tendency. —Translator's Note.

systems have foundered (leaving it in the end to philosophies subjugated by the science of phenomena to expel them), those notions, I say, cannot enter into a properly philosophical context and be justified in that context except from the point of view of an existentialist intellectualism like that of Thomas Aquinas. For no pure essence will ever be a cause or ever be an end. Efficient causality is an overflow into existence which supposes a tendency in beings thus to superabound existentially. And final causality is the reason for this overflow of beings into existence, and for the orientation of the tendency within them to surpass themselves existentially. This is why their causality is exercised only in virtue of that super-causality by which the activation of the First Existent penetrates them, and in virtue of that super-finality by which they love the separated common Good more than themselves and tend towards it (even though they be but birds, or moss, or inanimate molecules) more primordially and more intensely than towards their own specific end.

11. At this point there appears an aspect of Thomism which is in my opinion of first importance. By the very fact that the metaphysics of St. Thomas is centered, not upon essences but upon existence—upon the mysterious gushing forth of the act of existing in which, according to the analogical variety of the degrees of being, qualities and natures are actualised and formed, which qualities and natures refract and multiply the transcendent unity of subsistent Being itself in its created participations—this metaphysics lays hold, at its very starting point, of being as superabundant. Being superabounds every-

where; it scatters its gifts and fruits in profusion. This is the action in which all beings here below communicate with one another and in which, thanks to the divine influx that traverses them, they are at every instant—in this world of contingent existence and of unforeseeable future contingents—either better or worse than themselves and than the mere fact of their existence at a given moment. By this action they exchange their secrets, influence one another for good or ill, and contribute to or betray in one another the fecundity of being, the while they are carried along despite themselves in the torrent of divine governance from which nothing can escape.

Above time, in the primary and transcendent Source, it is the superabundance of the divine act of existing, superabundance in pure act, which manifests itself in God Himself (as revelation teaches us) by the plurality of the divine Persons, and (as reason is of itself qualified to know) by the fact that the very existence of God is Intelligence and is Love, and by the fact that this existence is freely creative. Moreover this divine plenitude does not merely give, it gives itself. And it was, in the last analysis, in order to give itself to spiritual beings apt to receive it that, specifically, it created the world. It is not for Himself but for us, St. Thomas says, that God made all things for His glory.

Now if being is superabundant and communicative of itself, if it gives itself, love is thereby justified; justified also is that *eros*, that natural love which is coextensive with being and which instils in all things, at every degree of being, an ineradicable and multiform propensity. Justified, too, that stimulation and that aspiration to emerge from self to share the very life of the beloved, which are con-

substantial with the human being and which no philosophy of pure essence is capable of recognising.
For a Spinoza the summit of wisdom and of human
perfection will be to love God *intellectually,* that is
to say, to consent, as a pure disinterested spectator,
to the universal order of things, without asking to be
loved in return, because Spinoza's God is but a subsistent essence. But for St. Thomas Aquinas the summit of wisdom and of human perfection was to love
lovingly the sovereignly personal principle of every
act of existing; not only to love it, but also—nay,
above all!—to be loved by it; in other words, to open
oneself to the plenitude of its love descending into
us and overflowing from us so that we may continue
through time its work and communicate its goodness.[31]

If love and propensity are coextensive with being;
if the good is an epiphany of being; if all things as-
pire; if all things are at grips with existence; if all
things pour out their being in action; if all things
strive, each after its own fashion, towards the subsistent Good which infinitely transcends them; if, in
all things, being and the transcendental properties
of being tend towards that plenitude which is higher
than any name, where all are identified in an intan-
gible life, and exist in pure act—is it not clear that the
philosophy of being is also, is identical with, the philosophy of the dynamism of being?—and is not all
this true because to exist is act *par excellence* and
because the Act of Existing, subsistent by itself, is
above the whole order of beings, perfections, exist-
ences which are its created participations and which
contrive together in its attraction and in its activa-

[31] Cf. J. Maritain, *De Bergson à Thomas d'Aquin,* pp.
312-334.

tion? Those who on the pretext that natures and intelligible structures and degrees of being exist for this philosophy, regard its conception of reality as 'static,' as they say, simply own that they do not know what they are talking about. Devoted to the mystery of the act of existing, this philosophy is by that very fact devoted to the mystery of action and the mystery of movement.

I do not question that St. Thomas Aquinas made no systematic use of the idea of development or evolution in the modern sense of these words. But, for one thing, that idea itself is neither enlightening nor fertile except in the context of an ontological analysis of reality. In claiming to take the place of such an analysis, and itself become the supreme explanatory principle, it does no more, as Goethe observed, than to exercise upon thought an infinite power of dissolution. For it is not a metaphysical instrument and it does not concern the analytical explanation of being; it is an historic instrument and concerns the historical explanation of becoming. For another thing, it is quite true that history was not the strong side of the Middle Ages, and that historical explanation was absent from the sciences of nature with which St. Thomas had to deal. That is a conquest of modern science. But to enclose a metaphysic in a compartment of history is not a way to give evidence of a sense of history; and it is no proof of philosophic sense to think that there is nothing more in a metaphysic than the scientific imagery which, in a given era, permitted it to exemplify itself in the plane of phenomena, which plane never in fact confined it. Not only is everything present in the equipment of Thomism to allow it to find room for the historic dimension in the knowledge of Nature and the knowledge of Man, but its primary intuitions await, so to say, the introduction into it of that dimension; they are eager to welcome and to carry out the idea of development and evolution, and to complete the *opus philosophicum* by a philosophy of history.

Chapter Two

ACTION

The Perfection of Human Life

12. Up to now we were concerned with metaphysics and speculative philosophy. I have pointed out that Thomism is an existentialist intellectualism. This, coupled with St. Thomas's insistence on the primacy of the speculative, illustrates the essential difference which sets this philosophy apart from contemporary existentialism as well as from every philosophy that proves false to its name by repudiating speculation in favor of action, and confusing knowledge with power.

In practical or ethical philosophy, with which we shall now deal, St. Thomas's existentialism retains the same intellectualist character, in the sense that practical philosophy remains speculative in its mode (since it is philosophy), although practical by reason of its object (which is moral conduct). Here again there are natures to be known—but this time they serve to constitute norms of conduct, since practical knowledge has for its purpose to guide action. In another sense, however, we must say that in moving into the domain of ethics this existentialism becomes voluntaristic. This is clear when we consider

the rôle which it assigns to the will (by which alone
a man can be made to be good or bad, in the pure
and absolute meaning of those terms) and the fact
that it makes the practical judgment dependent
upon the actual movement of the appetite towards
the ends of the subject.

Precisely because in ethics or practical philosophy
Thomist existentialism is ordered, not to the existence exercised by things, but to the act which the
liberty of the subject will bring into existence, the
differences in metaphysical point of view, profound
though they be, will nevertheless not preclude certain contacts between this existentialism and contemporary existentialism. As a matter of fact, it is in
the domain of moral philosophy that the views
which modern existentialism contributes seem to me
to be the most worthy of interest. However ill it may
conceive liberty, it does have an authentic feeling
for it and for its essential transcendence with regard to the specifications and virtualities of essence,
though they be those of the 'profound self.'[1] It has
a feeling also for the creative importance of the
moral act (creative, of course, in a relative sense),
and the degrees of depth which the moral act comports, as well as of the absolute uniqueness of the
instant (irreducible to any chain of anterior events
and determinations) when, by the exercise of his liberty, the subject is revealed to himself and 'committed.'[*] (Would that I could avoid using that word!
Yet the way in which it has been made a commonplace shows that its value is appreciated.) If all this
were not spoiled by the acceptance of absurdity and

[1] J. P. Sartre, *L'Etre et le Néant*, pp. 78-81.

[*] 'Committed' is our translation of M. Sartre's *engagé*.—
Translator's Note.

by the eviction of nature and the *forma rationis,* as well as of all object, all causality, and all finality, we should have here the premises of a moral philosophy and a philosophy of liberty.

As concerns the fundamentally existential character of Thomist[2] ethics, I shall confine myself to two significant and well-known doctrines.

The first relates to the perfection of human life. St. Thomas teaches that perfection consists in charity, and that each of us is bound to tend towards the perfection of love according to his condition and in so far as it is in his power. All morality thus hangs upon that which is most existential in the world. For love (this is another Thomist theme) does not deal with possibles or pure essences, it deals with existents. We do not love possibles, we love that which exists or is destined to exist. And in the last analysis it is because God is the Act of Existing Itself, in His ocean of all perfection, that the love of that which is better than all goodness is that in which man attains the perfection of his being. That perfection does not consist in reunion with an essence by means of supreme accuracy in copying the ideal; it consists in loving, in going through all that is unpredictable, dangerous, dark, demanding, and insensate in love; it consists in the plenitude and refinement of dia-

---

[2] Because of the fundamentally existential character of Thomist moral philosophy—however vast, necessary, and fundamental be the part that natural ethics plays in it—a moral philosophy adequately taken, that is, a moral philosophy really apt to guide action, is conceivable in such a philosophy only if it takes into account the existential state of humanity, with all the wounds or weaknesses and all the resources that it comprises in fact; and if, therefore, it takes into account the higher data of theology (as well as the data of ethnology and sociology). Cf. J. Maritain, *Science et Sagesse,* pp. 228-362, Eng. trans., pp. 138-220.

logue and union of person with person to the point of transfiguration which, as St. John of the Cross says, make of man a god by participation, 'two natures in a single spirit and love,' in a single spiritual super-existence of love.

Moral Judgment

13. The second point of doctrine, dominating the whole theory of the virtue of prudence in particular, concerns the judgment of the moral conscience and the manner in which, at the heart of concrete existence, the appetite enters into the regulation of the moral act by the reason. Here St. Thomas makes the rectitude of the intellect depend upon that of the will; and this because of the practical, not speculative, existentiality of the moral judgment. Not only is the truth of the practical intellect generally understood to be conformity with right appetite (not, as in the case of the speculative intellect, conformity with extramental being), because the end is not to know that which exists, but to cause that to exist which is not yet; but also the act of moral choice is so individualised (both by the singularity of the person from whom it emanates and by that of the context of contingent circumstance in which it takes place) that the practical judgment in which it is expressed and by which I declare to myself, 'This is what I need,' can only be right if actually, *hic et nunc*, the dynamism of my willing is right and tends towards the genuine goods of human life.

This is why practical wisdom, *prudentia*, is a virtue indivisibly moral and intellectual at the same time. This is why prudence, as, likewise, the judg-

ment of conscience, cannot be replaced by any sort
of science or theoretical knowledge.

The same moral case never appears twice in the
world. To speak absolutely strictly, precedent does
not exist. Each time, I find myself in a situation re-
quiring me to do a new thing, to bring into existence
an act that is unique in the world, an act which must
be in conformity with the moral law in a manner
and under conditions belonging strictly to me alone
and which have never arisen before. Useless to
thumb through the dictionary of cases of conscience!
Moral treatises will of course tell me the universal
rule or rules I am bound to apply; they will not tell
me how I, the unique I, am to apply them in the
unique context in which I am involved. No knowledge of moral essences, however perfect, meticu-
lous, or detailed it may be and however particularised those essences may be (though they will always
remain general); no casuistry, no chain of pure de-
duction, no science, can exempt me from my judgment of conscience, and, if I have some virtue, from
the exercise of the virtue of prudence, in which exercise it is the rectitude of my willing that has to
effect the accuracy of my vision. In the practical syllogism, the major, which enunciates the universal
rule, speaks only to the intellect; but the minor and
the conclusion are on a different plane; they are put
forward by the whole subject, whose intellect is
swept along towards the existential ends by which
(in virtue of his very liberty) his appetitive powers
are in fact subjugated.[3]

[3] There are in truth two practical syllogisms, one opening
into the speculativo-practical and the other into the practico-
practical. Take this as an example of the first: 'Murder is
forbidden by the Law. This act which attracts me is

There are objective norms of morality, there are duties and rules, because the measure of reason is the formal constitutive element of human morality. However, I neither apply them, nor apply them well, unless they are embodied in the ends which actually attract my desire and in the actual movement of my will. In many cases man finds himself confronted by simple rules, such as those which forbid homicide or adultery. They set him no problem except the problem of effectively following them. Yet, in order that a man follow them, at the moment of temptation they must not merely resound in his head as mere universal rules which suffice to condemn him though not to set him in motion; but he must recognise in them (by a kind of painful labour of intussusception and reflection upon himself) an urgent demand of his most highly individuated, most personal desire, for the ends upon which he has made his life depend. If not, he will not do the good he loves (loves inefficaciously, only because he sees it to be good in itself), but he will do the evil

---

murder. Therefore this act is forbidden by the Law.' The conclusion expresses the rule of reason, which I know and from which I turn away my eyes when I sin. This syllogism considers the act and its law; the subject does not enter, unless to be *submitted* to the universal as any individual *x* which forms part of the species.

The following is an example of the second syllogism: 'Murder is forbidden by the Law. This act which attracts me is murder, *and would cause me to deviate from what I love best*. Therefore *I shall not do it* (*and long live law!*).' Or it could be, contrariwise: 'Murder is forbidden by the Law. This act which attracts me is murder, *and I make it to be what I love best*. Therefore *I shall do it* (*and so much the worse for universal law!*).'

In the second syllogism it is the existential disposition of the subject in the free affirmation of his unique self which decides the question.

he does not wish to do (he does not wish it as evil, though he will at present make of it his good). But in many cases, which, in truth, form the stuff of our moral life, man finds himself confronted by a diversity of conflicting duties and multiple rules which crisscross in a context of circumstance where the problem 'What ought I really do?' is posed. This is the time when he must have recourse to the *regulae arbitrariae* of prudence; to those rules which not only take account of all the objective peculiarities of given conditions, but which become decisive only by reason of the subject's deepest attractions (which, by supposition, are duly orientated) and the inclinations of his virtues.

14. We are told, as if it were a novelty, that the motives which reason deliberates upon do not play the decisive part in the deepest, freest (indeed wisest) acts of moral option but that this rôle is reserved to that unforeseeable impulse of one's inscrutable subjectivity, so often disconcerting for the intellect of the subject himself. How can it be otherwise, if it is true that the judgment of the subject's conscience is obliged, at the moment when judgment is freely made, to take account also of the whole of the unknown reality within him—his secret capacities, his deeply rooted aspirations, the strength or frailty of his moral stuff, his virtues (if he has any), the mysterious call of his destiny? He cannot formulate any of these things. They are unknown to him in terms of reason. But the dim instinct he possesses of himself, and his virtue of prudence (if he has the virtues), know them without knowing it in the indescribable mode of cognition by connaturality. These are the elements of

evaluation (inexpressible in terms of notions) which are of highest account for the practical justness of the decision he will make when his will shall by its decision have rendered efficacious any objective motive vitally referred to all this inner world. Thus, the freest decision may appear to be a sheer result of fate—though rendered such by the actual exercise of free choice. The most prudent decision can sometimes appear irrational and inexplicable—its reasons being hidden in the substance of the subject. And when we subsequently recall the decision, being removed from the actual (though not conceptually perceptible) glow in which it was bathed, we may doubt retrospectively of its prudence and even of its freedom.

In the moral problems of which we speak, where we are obliged to reconcile contrasting virtues or duties, choice has to be made not only between good and evil but also, and usually, between the good and the better. It is at such a moment that we enter into the deepest arcana of moral life and that the individuality of the moral act assumes its supreme dimensions. St. Thomas teaches that the standard of the gifts of the Holy Ghost is higher than that of the moral virtues; that of the gift of counsel is higher than that of prudence. The saints always amaze us. Their virtues are freer than those of a merely virtuous man. Now and again, in circumstances outwardly alike, they act quite differently from the way in which a merely virtuous man acts. They are indulgent where he would be severe, severe where he would be indulgent. When a saint deserts her children or exposes them to rebellion in order to enter into religion; when another saint allows her brother to be assassinated at the monastery gate in order that there be no violation of the cloister; when a saint strips himself naked before his bishop out of love of poverty; when another chooses to be a beggar and shocks people by his vermin; when another abandons the duties of his status in society and becomes a galley slave out of love of the captives; when still another allows himself to be unjustly condemned rather than defend himself against a dishonorable accusation—they go beyond the mean. What does that signify? They have their own kind of mean, their own kinds of standards. But they are valid only for each one of them. Although their standards are higher than those of reason, it is not because of the object taken in itself that the act measured by their standards is better than an act measured by the mere moral virtues; rather it is so by the inner impetus which the saints receive from the Spirit of God in the depths of their incommunicable subjectivity, which impetus goes beyond the measure of reason to a higher good discerned by them alone, and to which they are called to bear witness. This is why there would be no saintliness in the world if all excess and all that reason judges insensate were removed from the world. This is why we utter something deeper than we realise when we say of such acts that they are admirable but not imitable. They are not generalisable, universalisable. They are good; indeed, they are the best of all moral acts. But they are good only for him who does them. We are here very far from the Kantian universal with its morality defined by the possibility of making the maxim of an act into a law for all men.

15. Kierkegaard's great error, amid all his great intuitions, was to separate and oppose as two hetero-

geneous worlds the world of *generality*, or universal law, and that of the unique witness (unjustifiable at the bar of human reason) borne by the 'knight of the faith.' Consequently, he had to sacrifice, or at least 'suspend' ethics. In reality these two worlds are in continuity; both form part of the universe of ethics, which itself is divided into typically diversified zones according to the degree of depth of moral life. They go from the ethical realm of animal man to the ethical realm of spiritual man and the pneuma; from the wholly superficial realm in which moral life is barely moral, barely integrated by conscience and consists in outward conformity with common opinion, with the rules and tabus of the social group, right to the extreme depths, hidden in the life divine, where moral life is fully moral and fully integrated by conscience, by the conscience of that *spiritualis homo* who judgeth all things and whom no man judgeth.[4] Not only a tragic hero like Agamemnon, but Abraham himself sacrificing Isaac still belongs to the universe of ethics. Abraham, stricken to the heart by the personal command of God and the contradiction by which he was torn, Abraham still had a universal law, the first of all laws: Thou shalt worship God, the Incomprehensible, and shalt obey Him. Abraham knew obscurely, not out of treatises on moral theology but by the instinct of the Holy Ghost, that the killing of his child was exempt from the law forbidding homicide, because it was commanded by the Master of life.[5]

Moreover, from the moment when ethical comportment is not a mere waking dream guided by the

---

[4] *Spiritualis autem judicat omnia: et ipse a nemine judicatur.* I Corinthians II, 15.

[5] Cf. *Sum. theol.*, II-II, 64, 6, *ad* 1.

fear of social penalties or the concern to justify oneself in the eyes of other men; from the moment when
man has truly crossed the threshold of moral life;
from that moment, as has already been indicated,
universal law is vitally interiorised, embowled, ex-
istentialised in the dynamism of the individual subject tending towards the ends which are of importance to him above all else. Even when a man obeys
the law as a slave to the law, because he wishes an
evil act but fears hell and the wrath of God still
more, this is not the mere logical subsuming of a particular case under a general law, the subsuming of
an anonymous act (connoting a casual *anybody*) under a rule which lays down what everybody is held
to do. It is his own fear, *his* fear ravaging *his* conscience, causing him to tremble lest he lose his soul,
that crushes his will to evil under the heel of the
law, and makes him identify the *self*, unique and
precious above all others, the *self* troubled and re-
bellious within the man he is, with the *everyman*
subjected to the universal precept.

When a man obeys the law in the manner of one
faithful to the law (because, desiring justice above
all else, he does not wish that evil act to which to-
day he is tempted and which the law forbids), it is
his own desire, deeper and stronger than that allur-
ing attraction, his own appetite for the ends he desires beyond all else and desires for himself—it is this
which harmonises his will with the law (since it remains a will to good) and makes him identify his
self with the *everyman* who is subject to the universal precept.

When he obeys the law as a friend of the law because the Spirit of God renders him one in spirit and
love with the Principle of the law, and does of his

own accord that which the law commands, he is no longer under the law; it is his own love, now sovereign and sovereignly free, his love of his God and his All, which causes him to obey the law that has now become his law, the personal call by which the word of Him he loves reaches him. This is a law in regard to which he is no longer a *self* to be identified with *everyman*. He is *this man* himself, this man answering to his own name, to whom the law speaks in his pure solitude with God.

When St. Thomas teaches us that the gifts of the Holy Ghost are given to all because they are necessary to salvation, he teaches us in the same breath that, at certain moments and at certain depths in the universe of ethics, each of us may have to make the sacrifice Abraham made and exceed the bounds of reason. (This, of course, does not mean that we shall thus be placed in the exceptional situation and the exceptional grandeur in which Abraham was placed.) And when St. Thomas teaches us, with regard to the universe of ethics as a whole, and in connection with the life of the practical reason and the mere moral virtues, that there is no exercise of the virtues without the personal judgment of prudence, and more generally that there is no moral life without the personal judgment of conscience, he teaches us thereby that in every authentically moral act, man, in order to apply and in applying the law, must embody and grasp the universal in his own singular existence, where he is alone face to face with God.

As for our contemporary atheistic existentialists, they reject the ethical universal along with all essence. They do not sacrifice it in pain and anguish, as Kierkegaard did, knowing its value the while. Rather they wantonly repudiate it with the pleasure

of barbarians and they know not what they do. As
a matter of fact they seem to think that if there were
a system of moral rules, those rules would apply to
particular cases automatically and of themselves.
Whence it would follow that all morality is in de-
fault. For it ought to suffice, yet does not suffice, for
a young friend of M. Sartre's, say, who hesitates to
join the Fighting French for fear of breaking his
mamma's heart, to consult a dictionary of precepts
of a moral system to find out what course he ought
to follow.

In a word, they imagine that morality exempts us
from conscience and substitutes its golden rules for
that flexible and delicate instrument (which costs us
so dear) and for its invincibly personal judgment.
They imagine that morality offers that same substitute also for the likewise invincibly personal judgment (which is irreducible to any kind of science)
of the virtue of prudence, whose cost is still more
disquietingly high. They replace all this by the
Pythia's chasm because they have thrown out reason and make the formal element of morality consist in pure liberty alone. Let the perplexed young
man go cock an ear at that hole of the oracle; his
liberty itself will tell him how to make use of liberty.

Above all, let no man give him counsel! The least
bit of advice comports the risk of causing his liberty
to wither, of preventing the handsome serpent from
crawling out of the hole. For the liberty of these philosophers of liberty is singularly fragile. In uprooting
it from reason they have themselves made an inva-
lid of it. But we for our part do not fear to counsel
human liberty. Cram it with advice as much as you
like, we know that it is strong enough to digest advice and that it thrives on rational motivations which

it bends as it pleases and which it alone can render efficacious. In short, by suppressing generality and universal law, you suppress liberty; and what you have left is nothing but that amorphous impulse surging out of the night which is but a false image of liberty. Because when you suppress generality and universal law, you suppress reason, in which liberty, whole and entire, has its root[6] and from which emanates in man so vast a desire that no motive in the world and no objective solicitation, except Beatitude seen face to face, suffices to determine it.[7]

[6] *Totius libertatis radix est in ratione constituta.* St. Thomas, *De Verit.*, 24, 2.

[7] Cf. J. Maritain, *De Bergson à Thomas d'Aquin*, Chap. V. ('The Thomist Idea of Liberty').

Chapter Three

THE EXISTENT

The Subject (*suppositum*)

16. I have spoken of the existential (practical-existential) character of the judgment of conscience whose truth is measured by the rightly orientated voluntary dynamism of the subject. It is time now to furnish a few indications concerning this very notion of subject and the place it occupies in the overall vision of Thomist philosophy. Precisely because of the existentialism (existentialist intellectualism) of this philosophy, the notion of subject plays a capital part in it; we may even say that *subjects* occupy all the room there is in the Thomist universe, in the sense that, for Thomism, only subjects exist, with the accidents which inhere in them, the action which emanates from them, and the relations which they bear to one another. Only individual subjects exercise the act of existing.

What we call *subject* St. Thomas called *suppositum*. Essence is *that which* a thing is; suppositum is *that which* has an essence, *that which* exercises existence and action—*actiones sunt suppositorum*—*that which* subsists. Here we meet the metaphysical notion which has given students so many headaches

and baffles everyone who has not grasped the true
—the existential—foundation of Thomist metaphysics, the notion of *subsistence*.

We are bound to speak of this notion of subsistence with great respect, not only because of the
transcendent applications made of it in theology, but
because, in the philosophical order itself, it bears
witness to the supreme tension of an articulated
thought bent on seizing intellectually something
which seems to escape from the world of notions or
ideas of the intellect, namely, the typical reality of
the subject. The existential subject has this in common with the act of existing, that both transcend the
concept or the idea considered as the terminus of
the first operation of mind or simple apprehension.
I have tried to show in an earlier section how the
intellect (because it envelops itself) grasps in an
idea which is the first of its ideas, that very thing,
the act of existing, which is the intelligible (or rather
the super-intelligible) proper to the judgment, and
not to simple apprehension. Now we are no longer
dealing with the act of existing but with that which
exercises that act. Just as there is nothing more commonplace in language than the word being (and this
is the greatest mystery of philosophy) so there is
nothing more commonplace than the 'subject' to
which in all our propositions we attribute a predicate. And when we undertake a metaphysical analysis of the reality of this subject, this individual thing
which maintains itself in existence, this supremely
concrete reality, and undertake to do justice to its
irreducible originality, we are forced to appeal to
that which is most abstract and most elaborate in
our lexicon of notions. How can we be astonished
that minds which are fond of facility should regard

as so many vain scholastic refinements and Chinese
puzzles the elucidations in which Cajetan and John
of St. Thomas show us that subsistence is distinct
both from essence and from existence, and describe
it as a substantial mode? I concede that the style of
their dissertations seems to carry us very far from
experience into the third heaven of abstraction. And
yet, in reality their aim was to form an *objective notion* of the *subject* itself or the suppositum, to reach
objectively, within the ontological analysis of the
structure of reality, the property which makes the
subject to be subject and not object, and to transcend, or rather exceed in depth, the whole universe
of objects.

When they explain that an essence or a nature,
considered strictly, cannot exist outside the mind as
an object of thought, and that nevertheless individual natures do exist, and that, consequently, in order
to exist, a given nature or essence must be other than
it has to be in order to be an object of thought, that
is to say, it must bear in itself a supreme achieve-
ment which adds nothing to it in the line of its essence (and consequently does not enrich our understanding by any new note which qualifies it), but
which *terminates* it in that line of essence (closes or
situates it, constitutes it as an *in-itself* or an inwardness face to face with existence) in order that it may
take possession of this act of existing for which it is
created and which transcends it;[1] when they explain

---

[1] Cf. the *Further Elucidations On the Notion of Subsistence* which I wrote for the new translation of *The Degrees
of Knowledge* (to be published by Scribner's in 1957).
Here are some excerpts from this essay:

"The *esse*, is perceived quite precisely—even as in their
own order intellection and volition—as an *exercised* act,
exercised by the thing or the existent subject, or as an

in this fashion *that by which,* on the plane of reality, the *quod* which exists and acts is other than the *quid* which we conceive, they attest the existential character of metaphysics, they shatter the Platonic world of pure objects, they justify the passage into the world of subjects or supposita, they rescue for the metaphysical intellect the value and reality of subjects.

---

activity in which the existent itself is engaged, an energy that it exerts. Existence is therefore not only received, as if by *esse* essences were pinned outside nothingness like a picture hung on a wall. Existence is not only received, it is also *exercised.* . . . But to *exercise* existence something besides the bare essence is necessary, namely the supposit or person. *Actiones sunt suppositorum,* actions are proper to supposits, and especially and above all the act of exercising existence. In other words, to exercise existence the essence must be completed by subsistence and thus become a supposit. . . . Since existence by its very notion demands, as we have just seen, that it be not only received but exercised, and since this exigency, pertaining as it does to the existential order, places us outside and beyond the order of essence, it must be said that (substantial) essence or nature can *receive* existence only by *exercising* it, which it cannot do as long as it remains in its own essential order. In other words, it can receive existence only on condition of being drawn at the same time from the state of simple essence and placed in an *existential state* which makes of it a *quod* capable of exercising existence. This *state* which completes, or rather surcompletes the essence—not at all in the line of essence itself, but in relation to a completely other order, the existential order—and permits the essence (henceforth supposit) to *exercise* existence is precisely subsistence. . . .

"So the proper effect of subsistence is to place the individual nature in a state of *exercising existence,* with the incommunicability proper to the individual nature. . . . This is the promotion onto a new plane of the incommunicability which defines singularity. Subsistence renders the essence (become supposit) capable of existing *per se separatim,* because it renders an individual nature (become supposit) capable of exercising existence."

17. God does not create essences to which He can be imagined as giving a last rub of the sandpaper of subsistence before sending them forth into existence! God creates existent subjects or supposita which subsist in the individual nature that constitutes them and which receive from the creative influx their nature as well as their subsistence, their existence, and their activity. Each of them possesses an essence and pours itself out in action. Each is, for us, in its individual existing reality, an inexhaustible well of knowability. We shall never know everything there is to know about the tiniest blade of grass or the least ripple in a stream. In the world of existence there are only subjects or supposita, and that which emanates from them into being. This is why ours is a world of nature and adventure, filled with events, contingency, chance, and where the course of events is flexible and mutable whereas the laws of essence are necessary. We know those subjects, we shall never get through knowing them. We do not know them as subjects, we know them by objectising them, by achieving objective insights of them and making them our objects; for the object is nothing other than something of the subject transferred into the state of immaterial existence of intellection in act. We know subjects not as subjects, but as objects, and therefore only in such-and-such of the intelligible aspects, or rather *inspects,* and perspectives in which they are rendered present to the mind and which we shall never get through discovering in them.

As we pass progressively to higher degrees in the scale of beings we deal with subjects of existence or supposita more and more rich in inner complexity, whose individuality is more and more concentrated and integrated, whose action manifests a more and more perfect spontaneity, from the merely transitive activity of inanimate bodies to the occultly immanent activity of vegetable life, the definitely immanent activity of sentient life, and the perfectly immanent activity of the life of the intellect.[2] At this last degree the threshold of free choice is crossed, and therewith the threshold of independence properly so-called (however imperfect it be) and of personality. With man, liberty of spontaneity becomes liberty of autonomy, the *suppositum* becomes *persona*, that is, a whole which subsists and exists in virtue of the very subsistence and existence of its spiritual soul, and acts by setting itself its own ends; a universe in itself; a microcosm which, though its existence at the heart of the material universe is ceaselessly threatened, nevertheless possesses a higher ontological density than that whole universe. Only the person is free; only the person possesses, in the full sense of these words, inwardness and subjectivity—because it contains itself and moves about within itself. The person, St. Thomas says, is that which is noblest and highest in all nature.

*

Subjectivity as subjectivity

18. By sense or experience, science or philosophy, each of us, as I said a moment ago, knows the environing world of subjects, supposita, and persons in their rôle as objects. The paradox of consciousness and personality is that each of us is situated precisely

[2] Cf. J. Maritain, *De Bergson à Thomas d'Aquin,* Chap. VI ('Spontaneity and Independence').

at the centre of this world. Each is at the centre of
infinity. And this privileged subject, the thinking
self, is to itself not object but subject; in the midst
of all the subjects which it knows only as objects, it
alone is subject as subject. We are thus confronted
by subjectivity as subjectivity.

I know myself as subject by consciousness and re-
flexivity, but my substance is obscure to me. St.
Thomas explains that in spontaneous reflection,
which is a prerogative of the life of the intellect, each
of us knows (by a kind of knowledge that is not scientific but experimental and incommunicable) that
his soul exists, knows the singular existence of this
subjectivity that perceives, suffers, loves, thinks.
When a man is awake to the intuition of being he is
awake at the same time to the intuition of subjectivity; he grasps, in a flash that will never be
dimmed, the fact that *he is a self*, as Jean-Paul said.
The force of such a perception may be so great as
to sweep him along to that heroic asceticism of the
void and of annihilation in which he will achieve
ecstasy in the substantial existence of the *self* and
the 'presence of immensity' of the divine Self at one
and the same time—which in my view characterises
the natural mysticism of India.[3]

But the intuition of subjectivity is an existential
intuition which surrenders no essence to us. We
know *that which* we are by our phenomena, our
operations, our flow of consciousness. The more we
grow accustomed to the inner life, the better we de-
cipher the astonishing and fluid multiplicity which
is thus delivered to us; the more, also, we feel that

[3] Cf. J. Maritain, *Quatre essais sur l'Esprit dans sa condition charnelle,* Chap. III ('Natural Mystical Experience
and the Vacuum').

it leaves us ignorant of the essence of our self. Subjectivity *as subjectivity* is inconceptualisable; is an unknowable abyss. It is unknowable by the mode of notion, concept, or representation, or by any mode of any science whatsoever—introspection, psychology, or philosophy. How could it be otherwise, seeing that every reality known through a concept, a notion, or a representation is known as object and not as subject? Subjectivity as such escapes by definition from that which we know about ourselves by means of notions.

19. Yet it is known in a way, or rather in certain ways, which I should like briefly to enumerate. At the very beginning and above all, subjectivity is known or rather felt in virtue of a formless and diffuse knowledge which, in relation to reflective consciousness, we may call unconscious or pre-conscious knowledge. This is knowledge of the 'concomitant' or spontaneous consciousness, which, without giving rise to a distinct act of thought, envelops in fact, *in actu exercito,* our inner world in so far as it is integrated into the vital activity of our spiritual faculties.[4] Even for the most superficial persons, it is true that from the moment when they say *I*, the whole unfolding of their states of consciousness and their operations, their musings, memories, and acts, is subsumed by a virtual and ineffable knowledge, a vital and existential knowledge of the totality immanent in each of its parts, and immersed, without their troubling to become aware of it, in the diffuse glow, the unique freshness, the maternal connivance as it were, which emanates from subjectivity. Sub-

---

[4] Cf. J. Maritain, *De Bergson à Thomas d'Aquin,* pp. 160-161.

jectivity is not known, it is felt as a propitious and enveloping night.

There is, secondly, a knowledge of subjectivity as such, imperfect and fragmentary of course, but in this instance formed and actually given to the mind, and which is thrown into relief by what St. Thomas calls knowledge by mode of inclination, sympathy, or connaturality, not by mode of knowledge. It appears before us under three specifically distinct forms: (1) practical knowledge, which judges both moral matters and the subject itself, by the inner inclinations of the subject. I mentioned this some pages back in connection with moral conscience and prudence; (2) poetic knowledge, in which subjectivity and the things of this world are known together in creative intuition-emotion and are revealed and expressed together, not in a word or concept but in a created work;[5] (3) mystical knowledge, which is not directed towards the subject but towards things divine, and does not of itself issue in any expression, but in which God is known by union and by connaturality of love, and in which this very love that becomes the formal means of knowledge of the divine Self, simultaneously renders the human self transparent in its spiritual depths. Let the mystic reflect an instant upon himself, and a St. Theresa or a St. John of the Cross will show us to what extent the divine light gives him a lucid and inexhaustible knowledge of his own subjectivity.

But in none of these instances is the knowledge of subjectivity as subjectivity, however real it be, a knowledge by mode of knowledge, which is to say, by mode of conceptual objectisation.

[5] Cf. Jacques and Raïssa Maritain, *Situation de la poésie*, Paris, 1947.

20. In none of these instances is it philosophical knowledge. It would be a contradiction in terms to seek to make a philosophy of that sort of knowledge, since every philosophy—like it or not—proceeds by concepts. This is the first point to which the consideration of subjectivity as subjectivity draws our attention; and it is a point of capital importance. Subjectivity marks the frontier which separates the world of philosophy from the world of religion. This is what Kierkegaard felt so deeply in his polemic against Hegel. Philosophy runs against an insurmountable barrier in attempting to deal with subjectivity, because while philosophy of course knows subjects, it knows them only as objects. Philosophy is registered whole and entire in the relation of intelligence to object; whereas religion enters into the relation of subject to subject. For this reason, every philosophical religion, or every philosophy which, like Hegel's, claims to assume and integrate religion into itself, is in the last analysis a mystification.

When philosophy, taking its start in the being of things, attains to God as the cause of being, it has then, thanks to ana-noetic knowledge,[6] rendered the divine Self an object of philosophical knowledge expressed in concepts. These concepts do not circumscribe the supreme reality presented by them. On the contrary, that divine reality infinitely overflows the banks of conceptual knowledge. But philosophy knows thereby, or ought to know, that the reality thus objectised 'through a glass, darkly,' is the reality of a transcendent Self inscrutable in its being and its goodness, in its liberty and its glory. And all the other intelligent *selves* who know it, from the in-

[6] Cf. *Les Degrés du savoir*, pp. 432-447, Eng. trans., pp. 268-278.

stant that they do know it, owe to it, as their first
duty, obedience and adoration. St. Paul blamed pa-
gan wisdom for not recognising that glory of God of
which it was in fact aware. But in fact, to recognise
that glory is already to adore it. It is something to
know that God is a transcendent and sovereign
Self; but it is something else again to enter oneself
and with all one's baggage—one's own existence and
flesh and blood—into the vital relationship in which
created subjectivity is brought face to face with this
transcendent subjectivity and, trembling and loving,
looks to it for salvation. This is the business of religion.

Religion is essentially that which no philosophy
can be: a relation of person to person with all the
risk, the mystery, the dread, the confidence, the de-
light, and the torment that lie in such a relationship.
And this very relationship of subject to subject[7] demands that into the knowledge of uncreated subjectivity which the created subjectivity possesses there
shall be transferred something of that which the latter is as *subjectivity*, i.e., as that uncreated subjectivity is in the mystery of its personal life. Whence all
religion comports an element of revelation. Therefore in the true faith it is the First Truth in Person which makes known to man the mystery of
the divine subjectivity: *unigenitus filius, qui est*

[7] Is it necessary to explain that when we employ the word
subject in speaking of God, we do not do so in the sense
in which this word signifies receptivity as regards forms or
accidents (for in this sense God is obviously not a 'subject':
cf. *Sum. theol.*, I, q. 3, a. 6 and 7), but in the sense in
which, as the moderns employ it, the word signifies subsistence and Self. In this circumstance the word *subject* is
like the word *hypostasis* which has a similar etymology and
which is predicated formally-eminently of God (cf. *Sum.
theol.*, I, q. 29, a. 3).

in sinu patris, ipse enarravit.[8] This knowledge is still 'through a glass, darkly,' and therein the divine subjectivity is still objectised in order to be grasped by us. But this time it is in the glass of the super-analogy of faith,[9] in concepts which God Himself has chosen as His means of speaking to us about Himself—until at the last every glass falls away and then we know truly as we are known. Then shall we truly know the divine subjectivity as subjectivity in the vision in which the divine essence itself actuates our intellect and transports us in ecstasy within itself. While awaiting this state, the connaturality of love gives us, in apophatic contemplation, a dim sort of substitute and obscure foretaste of such a union.

21. Generally speaking, to *situate* the privileged subject which knows itself as subject in respect of all other subjects, which it knows as objects; to situate the self, that thinking reed in the crowd of thinking reeds, sets a singular problem. Each of us is able to say with Mr. Somerset Maugham: 'To myself I am the most important person in the world; though I do not forget that, not even taking into consideration so grand a conception as the Absolute, but from the standpoint of common sense, I am of no consequence whatever. It would have made small difference to the universe if I had never existed.'[10] This is a simple remark; but its implications are very wide.

Being the only subject which is a subject for me in the midst of a world of subjects which my senses and my intelligence can know only as objects, I am

[8] John I, 18.

[9] Cf. *Les Degrés du savoir*, pp. 478-484, Eng. trans., pp. 297-301.

[10] W. Somerset Maugham, *The Summing Up*, 1938, § 5.

at the centre of the world, as we observed a moment ago. With regard to my subjectivity in act, I *am* the centre of the world ('the most important person in the world'). My destiny is the most important of all destinies. Worthless as I know myself to be, I am more interesting than all the saints. There is me, and there are all the others. Whatever happens to the others is a mere incident in the picture; but what happens to me, what I myself have to do, is of absolute importance.

And yet, as regards the world itself, from the most obvious 'standpoint of common sense,' I know perfectly well that 'I am of no consequence whatever' and that 'it would have made small difference to the universe if I had never existed.' I know that I am one of the herd, not better than the rest, worth no more than the rest. I shall have been a tiny crest of foam, here one moment, gone in the twinkling of an eye, on the ocean of nature and humanity.

These two images—of myself and of my situation in respect of other subjects—can positively not be superposed. These two perspectives cannot be made to coincide. I oscillate rather miserably between them. If I abandon myself to the perspective of subjectivity, I absorb everything into myself, and, sacrificing everything to my uniqueness, I am riveted to the absolute of selfishness and pride. If I abandon myself to the perspective of objectivity, I am absorbed into everything, and, dissolving into the world, I am false to my uniqueness and resign my destiny. It is only from above that the antinomy can be resolved. If God exists, then not I, but He is the centre; and this time not in relation to a certain particular perspective, like that in which each created subjectivity is the centre of the universe it knows, but speaking absolutely, and as transcendent subjectivity to which all subjectivities are referred. At such time I can know both that I am without importance and that my destiny is of the highest importance. I can know this without falling into pride, know it without being false to my uniqueness. Because, loving the divine Subject more than myself, it is for Him that I love myself, it is to do as He wishes that I wish above all else to accomplish my destiny; and because, unimportant as I am in the world, I am important to Him; not only I, but all the other subjectivities whose lovableness is revealed in Him and for Him and which are henceforward, together with me, a *we*, called to rejoice in His life.

22. I am known to other men. They know me as object, not as subject. They are unaware of my subjectivity as such; unaware not merely of its inexhaustible depth, but also of that presence of the whole in each of its operations, that existential complexity of inner circumstances, data of nature, free choice, attractions, weaknesses, virtues perhaps, loves and pains; that atmosphere of immanent vitality which alone lends meaning to each of my acts. To be known as object, to be known to others, to see oneself in the eyes of one's neighbour (here M. Sartre is right) is to be severed from oneself and wounded in one's identity. It is to be always unjustly known—whether the *he* whom they see condemns the *I*, or whether, as occurs more rarely, the 'he' does honour to the 'I.' A tribunal is a masquerade where the accused stands accoutered in a travesty of himself, and *it* delivers his acts to be weighed in the balance. The more the judges stray from the crude outward criteria with which formerly they contented

themselves, and strive to take account of degrees of inner responsibility, the more they reveal that the truth of him whom they judge remains unknowable to human justice. Interrogated by such a tribunal, Jesus owed it to Himself to remain silent.

I am known to God. He knows all of me, me as subject. I am present to Him in my subjectivity itself; He has no need to objectise me in order to know me. Then, and in this unique instance, man is known not as object but as subject in all the depth and all the recesses of subjectivity. Only God knows me in this wise; to Him alone am I uncovered. I am not uncovered to myself. The more I know of my subjectivity, the more it remains obscure to me. If I were not known to God, no one would know me. No one would know me in my truth, in my own existence. No one would know me—*me*—as subject.

What this comes to is that no one would render justice to my being.[11] There could be no justice for me anywhere. My existence would be immersed in the injustice of the knowledge of me possessed by all the others and by the world itself; and in my own ignorance of myself. But if there is no justice possible with regard to my being, then there is no possible hope for me. If man is not known to God, and if he has the profound experience of his personal existence and his subjectivity, then he has also the ex-

---

[11] ' "You're tying yourself up more and more," said the Head Waiter. "If we're to believe you, we've got to keep forgetting what you said before.". . .
    ' "It's impossible to defend oneself where there is no good will," Karl told himself, and he made no further answer. . . . He knew that all he could say would appear quite different to the others, and that whether a good or a bad construction was to be put on his actions depended alone on the spirit in which he was judged.' Franz Kafka, *Amerika*, New York, 1946, p. 174 (English translation by Edwin Muir).

perience of his desperate solitude; and the longing
for death—more than this, the aspiration to total annihilation, is the sole spring that can gush forth
within him.

Finally, to know that I am known as subject in all
the dimensions of my being is not only to know that
my truth is known, and that in this knowledge justice is done me; it is also to know that I am *understood*. Even though God condemn me, I know that
He understands me. The idea that we are known to
Him who scrutinises the loins and the heart dissolves
us at first in fear and trembling because of the evil
that is within us. But on deeper reflection, how can
we keep from thinking that God Who knows us and
knows all those poor beings who jostle us and whom
we know as objects, whose wretchedness we mostly
perceive—how can we keep from thinking that God
Who knows all these in their subjectivity, in the
nakedness of their wounds and their secret evil,
must know also the secret beauty of that nature
which He has bestowed upon them, the slightest
sparks of good and liberty they give forth, all the
travail and the impulses of good-will that they drag
from the womb to the grave, the recesses of goodness
of which they themselves have no notion? The exhaustive knowledge possessed by God is a loving
knowledge. To know that we are known to God is
not merely to experience justice, it is also to experience mercy.

23. In any case, what I should like to say is that
our acts are tolerable to ourselves only because our
consciousness of them is immersed in the obscure experience of subjectivity. Our acts are hatched in it as
in a nest where everything, even the worst rendings

and the worst shames, connives with us to emanate
from us in the unique freshness of the present instant
that we are living. They bathe in that maternal atmosphere emanating from subjectivity, of which I
spoke earlier. There is nothing which crushes us so
much as our own acts when, forgotten and then one
day evoked by some relic of past time, they pass to
the state of objects, separated from the living waters
of subjectivity. Even if they were not specifically
evil, we are no longer sure that they were good and
that some unknown illusion or hidden impurity had
not tainted them—those strangers who fling themselves upon us like the dead come forth from within
to bring doubt and death to us.

It must be one of the natural features of the state
of damnation that the subject, not seeing himself in
God, and therefore not seeing his whole life in the
eternal instant to which everything is present, all his
good and evil acts come back upon him in the sterile
endlessly questioning light of the memory of the
dead, like enemy objects wholly detached from the
actual existence in which subjectivity is definitively
set, in the solitude of its ill-will which renders its own
past a separate thing for it.

But when the subject reaches his end and sees
himself in God and in divine eternity, all the moments of his past life are known to him in the actuality and the presentness of the instant in which they
were lived, and all his acts (even the evil, now not
only forgiven but leaving no spot nor shadow) are
known as emanating presently out of the freshness
of subjectivity, now itself become trans-luminous.
And in the virtue of the vision in which his intelligence possesses the *Ipsum esse subsistens* he knows
not only himself and all his life in a sovereignly ex-

istential manner, but also the other creatures whom in God he knows at last as subjects in the unveiled depth of their being.

The Structure of the Subject

24. To objectise is to universalise. The intelligibles in which a subject objectises itself for our mind are universal natures. It is in relation to the individuality itself of the subject (which the intelligence is not capable of grasping directly); in relation to its subjectivity as subjectivity, as something unique and singular, incommunicable and unconceptualisable, and in relation also to the subject's own experience of its own subjectivity, that objectisation is false to the subject and that, known as object, it is unjustly known, as we have already observed. On the other hand, in relation to its essential structures, the subject is in no wise betrayed when it is made object. The objectisation which universalises it and discerns in it intelligible natures, makes it known by a knowledge destined doubtless to continue to deepen, but not one that is in any sense unjust. Such a knowledge does no violence to the truth of the subject, but renders that truth present to the mind.

The subject, or suppositum, or person has an essence, an essential structure. It is a substance equipped with properties and which is acted upon and acts by the instrumentality of its potencies. The person is a substance whose substantial form is a spiritual soul; a substance which lives a life that is not merely biological and instinctive, but is also a life of intellect and will. It is a very simple-minded error to believe that subjectivity possesses no intelli-

gible structure, on the ground that it is an inexhaustible depth; and to conceive of it as without
any nature whatsoever for the purpose of making
of it an absurd abyss of pure and formless liberty.

These observations allow us to understand why
many contemporary philosophers, while they talk of
nothing but person and subjectivity, nevertheless
radically misunderstand those words. They remain
lightheartedly ignorant of the metaphysical problem of that *subsistence* concerning which something
was said in a preceding section. They do not see that
personality, metaphysically considered, being the
subsistence of the spiritual soul communicated to the
human composite, and enabling the latter to possess
its existence, to perfect itself and to give itself freely,
bears witness in us to the generosity or expansivity
of being which, in an incarnate spirit, proceeds from
the spirit and which constitutes, in the secret springs
of our ontological structure, a source of dynamic
unity and unification from within.[12]

Because analysis wearies them, they are ignorant
of what the proper life of the intelligence consists in,
and in what the proper life of the will consists. They
do not see that, because his *spirit* makes man cross
the threshold of independence properly so-called,
and of self-inwardness, the subjectivity of the person
demands as its most intimate privilege communica-
tions proper to love and intelligence. They do not
see that, even before the exercise of free choice, and
in order to make free choice possible, the most
deeply rooted need of the person is to communicate
with *the other* by the union of the intelligence, and

[12] Cf. J. Maritain, *La Personne et le Bien commun*, Paris,
1947, p. 34 (Eng. trans., N. Y., 1947, p. 31).

with *others* by the affective union. Their subjectivity is not a *self*, because it is wholly phenomenal.

25. I have already cited St. Thomas's aphorism, that the whole root of liberty is established in the reason. What reveals subjectivity to itself is not an irrational break (however profound and gratuitous it may be) in an irrational flow of moral and psychological phenomena, of dreams, automatisms, urges, and images surging upwards from the unconscious. Neither is it the anguish of forced choice. It is self-mastery for the purpose of self-giving. When a man has the obscure intuition of subjectivity, the reality, whose sudden invasion of his consciousness he experiences, is that of a secret totality, which contains both itself and its upsurge, and which superabounds in knowledge and in love. Only by love does it attain to its supreme level of existence—existence as self-giving.

'This is what I mean: Self-knowledge as a mere psychological analysis of phenomena more or less superficial, a wandering through images and memories, is but an egotistic awareness, however valuable it may be. But when it becomes ontological, then knowledge of the Self is transfigured, implying intuition of Being and the discovery of the actual abyss of subjectivity. At the same time, it is the discovery of the basic generosity of existence. Subjectivity, this essentially dynamic, living and open centre, both receives and gives. It receives through the intellect, by superexisting in knowledge. It gives through the will, by superexisting in love; that is, by having within itself other beings as inner attractions directed towards them and giving oneself to them, and by spiritually existing in the manner of a gift. And "it is better to give than to receive." The spiritual existence of love is the supreme revelation of existence for the Self. The Self, being not only a material individual but also a spiritual personality, possesses itself and holds itself in hand in so far as it is spiritual and in so far as it is free. And to what purpose does it possess itself and dispose of itself, if not for what *is better*, in actual existence and absolutely speaking, or to give of itself? Thus it is that when a man has been really awakened to the sense of being or existence, and grasps intuitively the obscure, living depth of the Self and subjectivity, he discovers by the same token the basic generosity of existence and realises, by virtue of the inner dynamism of this intuition, that love is not a passing pleasure or emotion, but the very meaning of his being alive.'[13]

By love, finally, is shattered the impossibility of knowing another except as object. I have emphasised this impossibility above at length and noted that it directly concerns the senses and the intellect. To say that union in love makes the being we love another *ourself* for us is to say that it makes that being another subjectivity for us, another subjectivity that is ours. To the degree that we truly love (which is to say, not for ourselves but for the beloved; and when—which is not always the case—the intellect within us becomes passive as regards love, and, allowing its concepts to slumber, thereby renders love a formal means of knowledge), to this degree we acquire an obscure knowledge of the being we love, similar to that which we possess of ourselves; we

[13] Cf. J. Maritain, 'A New Approach to God,' in *Our Emergent Civilization,* ed. by Ruth Nanda Anshen, Harper & Bros., N. Y., 1947, pp. 285-286. By permission of the publishers.

know that being in his very subjectivity (at least in a certain measure) by this experience of union. Then he himself is, in a certain degree, cured of his solitude; he can, though still disquieted, rest for a moment in the nest of the knowledge that we possess of him as subject.

Chapter Four

THE FREE EXISTENT AND
THE FREE ETERNAL PURPOSES

Time and Eternity

26. Linked to the considerations which held our attention in the preceding chapter (those considerations concerning the subject, the *existent*, the suppositum which possesses or exercises existence) is a problem, or rather the highest and most awesome mystery, with which the sciences that 'lisp of things divine' have to deal, namely, the problem of the relation between the liberty of the created existent and the eternal purposes of uncreated Liberty. That problem is of particular concern to theology. The theologian states it in terms of predestination to glory and reprobation, of sufficient grace and efficacious grace, of antecedent divine will and consequent divine will. It also concerns metaphysics, in a certain manner. For already in the natural order, the question of the relation between these two liberties arises. And for metaphysics it seems to me to present itself first of all in the following terms: What is the situation of man and of his fallible liberty in face of the absolutely free and absolutely immutable eternal plan established by the Uncreated in respect of the created? It is from this point of view that I shall

deal with it here by summarising as briefly as I can
my reflections upon Thomist principles continued
over many years. In order to make as clear as possible an exposition in which many and divers questions influence one another reciprocally, I must classify the points of which I shall treat under a certain
number of considerations.

First consideration: *Relation between time and
eternity.* Each moment of time is present to divine
eternity not only as being known to it, but 'physically' or in its being itself. John of St. Thomas has
established his master's doctrine on this point very
clearly.[1] All the moments of time are present to divine eternity—in which there is no succession, and
which is an instant that endures without beginning
or end—because the creative ideas embrace according to their own measure, which is eternity and
which infinitely transcends time, the created beings
which they cause to be, the proper measure of which
is the succession of time. 'This divine to-day is the
incommutable, indefeasible, inaccessible eternity to
which nothing can be added, from which nothing
can be taken away. And all things which here below
supervene upon and succeed one another by flowing
progressively into non-being, and which are diversified according to the vicissitudes of their times, are
present before this to-day and continue to exist mo-
tionless before it. In that to-day, the day when the
world began is still immutable. And nevertheless,

---

[1] Joannis a S. Thoma, *Cursus Theologicus*, (Vivès ed.
Paris, 1883-1886) Tome II, Quaest. X, Disp. 9, Art. 3, pp.
80-102; (Solesmes ed. Paris, 1931-) Tome II. In Quaest. X.
Iae P., Disp. 9, Art. 3, pp. 64-80.

the day is already present also when it will be
judged by the eternal judge.'[2]

Eternity contains and measures all time by possessing it in an indivisible manner. Thus any future
event, which in itself and in its own duration does
not yet exist, is already actually present in eternity
with all the events that preceded it and all the
events that will follow it. They are all there as terms
of the creative action which, without a shadow of
succession, causes them to occur successively and as
indivisibly possessed and measured by the eternal
instant which is the duration belonging properly to
that action. There is no future thing for God.[3]

It follows from this that, properly speaking, God
does not foresee the things of time, he sees them;
and he sees in particular the free options and deci-
sions of the created existent which, in as much as
they are free, are absolutely unforeseeable. He sees
them in the very instant when they take place, in
the pure existential freshness of their emergence
into being, in the humility of their own instant of
coming forth.

The Line of Good and the Line of Evil

27. Second consideration: *Liberty of the created
existent and the line of good.* If it is true, as has been
said in a preceding section, that no created cause
acts unless by virtue of the super-causality of the
Ipsum esse per se subsistens, if it is also true that
freedom of choice consists in the active and dominat-

[2] St. Peter Damien, Opusculum *De Divina Omnipotentia,*
cap. 8. P.L. 145,607.

[3] Cf. St. Thomas. In I Dist. 38, q. 1, art. 5.

ing indetermination of the will which itself renders efficacious the motive which determines it, then it is clear that the liberty of the created existent can be exercised only if it is activated or moved, penetrated to its depths and in the integrity of its determinations, by the influx of transcendent causality by which creative Liberty moves each created existent to act according to its own mode. That is to say, it activates to act necessarily, those which are subject to necessary determinations, contingently those which are subject to contingent determinations, and freely those whose act is subject to no sort of determination at all, unless it be that which it bestows upon itself.

There is no difficulty here that can obstruct thought, so long as the mind maintains itself in an existential perspective and provided it knows what transcendence and analogy mean. Consequently, in the existential subordination of causes, the created existent possesses *the whole* initiative of good, but this initiative is *second;* creative Liberty possesses the *whole* initiative of good and its initiative is *first*. There is not in the world a shadow of beauty, a trace of actuality, a spark of being of which the subsistent Being itself is not the author. The more so where it is a question of that singular nobility and ultimate flowering of being which is the morally good act of the free will.

Metaphysics, therefore, would not find itself faced with any major difficulty if the created existent always exercised its liberty in the line of good. But we know well enough that this is not the case.

28. Third consideration: *Dissymmetry between the line of good and the line of evil*. This dissymme-

try consists in the fact that whatever concerns the line of good is presented in terms of being, whereas whatever concerns the line of evil (I do not say, of evil action, for every action, in so far as it comports act or being, contains [metaphysical] good) whatever concerns the line of *evil as such* is presented in terms of *non-being,* of nothingness or of nihilation. For evil as such is a *privation,* that is to say, not only a mere absence of a good, a mere lacuna, or any sort of nothingness, but the absence of a *due* good, the nothingness of a form of being *requisite* to a given being; and the evil of the free act is the privation of due ruling* and form. This is what vitiates and wounds with nothingness, the use of liberty in the free act.

It follows from this that we cannot reason about the line of evil in the same way as we do about the line of good, nor can we apply indiscriminately to the former theses established in relation to the latter. The perspective has to be reversed; we have to think in terms of *nihil* instead of thinking in terms of *esse.*

29. Fourth consideration: *Liberty of the created existent and the line of evil.* What is the metaphysical root or pre-condition of evil in the free act? If that act is evil, that is to say wounded or corroded by nothingness, the reason is that before producing it, the will from which it emanates has already in some fashion withdrawn from being. It has done this freely, but without having as yet acted, or acted evilly (otherwise we should be in a vicious circle, and the fissure which we are seeking, through which

* In the sense in which we call bad conduct 'unruly' because it lacks conformity to the appropriate 'rule.'—Translator's Note.

evil introduces itself into the free act, and makes it evil, would already be a wicked act).

In one of his most difficult and most original theses, Thomas Aquinas explains[4] on this point that the emergence of a free and evil act resolves into two moments—distinct, not according to the priority of time, but according to an ontological priority. At a first moment there is in the will, by the fact of its very liberty, an absence or a nihilation which is not yet a *privation* or an evil, but a mere lacuna: the existent *does not* consider the norm of the *thou shouldst* upon which the ruling of the act depends. At a second moment the will produces its free act affected by the privation of its due ruling and wounded with the nothingness which results from this lack of consideration.

It is at this second moment that there is moral evil or sin. At the first moment there had not yet been moral fault or sin, but only the fissure through which evil introduces itself into the free decision about to come forth from the person, the vacuum or lacuna through which sin will take form in the free will before being launched into the arteries of the subject and of the world. This vacuum or lacuna, which St. Thomas calls non-consideration of the rule, is not an evil or a privation, but a mere lack, a mere nothingness of consideration. For of itself, it is not a duty for the will to consider the rule; that duty arises only at the moment of action, of production of being, at which time the will begets the free decision in which it *makes* its choice. Non-consideration of the rule becomes an evil, or becomes the privation of a good

---

[4] Cf. J. Maritain, *St. Thomas and the Problem of Evil,* The Aquinas Lectures, Milwaukee, 1942. (French text in *De Bergson à Thomas d'Aquin,* Chap. VII.)

that is due, only at the second of the two moments
we have distinguished—at the moment when the
will produces some act or some being; at the moment
when it causes the choice to irrupt; at the moment
when the free act is posited, with the wound or de-
formity of that non-consideration.

And still, without as yet being an evil or a fault,
that vacuum or lacuna, that non-consideration of the
rule, was already free; for it depends upon the freedom of the will to look or not to look at the rule. The
will has not acted, has not looked. And St. Thomas
says that the freedom of the will sufficiently accounts
for the fact that the will has not looked at the rule
and there is no need to seek farther. *Ad hoc sufficit
ipsa libertas voluntatis.*[5] We are faced here by an
absolute beginning which is not a beginning but a
'naught,' a fissure, a lacuna introduced into the warp
and woof of being. And we must henceforward do
violence to all the words in the language, for they
are all constructed in function of being and yet must
now be related, in an inevitably paradoxical form,
to the domain and the works of non-being and nothingness. The first cause (which is not an acting or
efficient cause, but is dis-acting and de-efficient),
the first cause of the non-consideration of the rule,
and consequently of the evil of the free act that will
come forth from it, is purely and simply the liberty
of the created existent.[6] The latter possesses the free
initiative of an absence (or 'nothingness') of consideration, of a vacuum introduced into the warp
and woof of being, of a *nihil;* and this time this free

---

[5] *De Malo*, q. 1, a. 3.

[6] Cf. *Sum. theol.*, I-II, 79, 2, *ad* 2: 'Homo est causa peccati'; and, *Ibid.*, 112, 3, *ad* 2: 'Defectus gratiae *prima causa*
est ex nobis.'

initiative is a *first* initiative because it does not consist in acting freely or allowing being to pass, but in freely not-acting and not-willing, in freely frustrating the passage of being.

It follows from this that whereas the created existent is never alone when it exercises its liberty in the line of good, and has need of the first cause for all that it produces in the way of being and of good, contrariwise, it has no need of God, it is truly alone, for the purpose of freely nihilating, of taking the free first initiative of this absence (or 'nothingness') of consideration, which is the matrix of the evil in the free act—I mean to say, the matrix of the *privation* itself by which the free act (in which there is metaphysical good in so far as there is being) is morally deformed or purely and simply evil. 'For without Me, you can do nothing';[7] which is to say, 'Without Me you can make that thing which is nothing.'

The Divine Activations

30. Fifth consideration: *Shatterable divine activations and unshatterable divine activations.* I have spoken of a void or vacuum introduced into the warp and woof of being. The reason is that I was considering the created existent as traversed and activated by all the influxes of being which derive from the *Ipsum esse subsistens* (whether they activate the created existent by whatsoever in the world incites to good in any way at all, or whether they activate it directly, as inspiration received from God by way of the intellect and the will, or as an impetus from

[7] John XV, 5.

the perpetual divine irradiation which prompts freedom to good acts). These influxes tend in each existent to bear it forward to the fulness of its being.
If it nihilates under their touch, if it non-acts, if it
adopts the free initiative of non-consideration, that
initiative creates a vacuum in the warp and woof of
being or of the influxes which are the bearers of being. In such case the existent frustrates, nihilates,
renders sterile—not actively, but by way of non-act-
ing—the divine activations which it has received.

Therefore if, in the world, we find moral evil and
free evil acts, the reason is that there are shatterable
divine activations. In other words, the reason is that
the First Cause sends down into free existents activations or motions which contain within themselves,
in advance, the permission or possibility of being
rendered sterile *if* the free existent which receives
them takes the first initiative of evading them, of
not-acting and not-considering, or nihilating under
their touch. And if it is true that every created liberty is by nature a fallible liberty[8] (since it is not its
own rule), if it is true that God activates all things,
each according to its own mode, if it is true that
creative Liberty, therefore, activates created liberties according to the fallible mode proper to them,
then we can understand that, in accordance with the
natural order of things, before the *unshatterable* divine activation, by which the will to good of creative
Liberty infallibly produces its effect in the created
will, the divine activations received by the free existent must first be *shatterable* activations.

It depends solely upon ourselves to shatter them
by making, upon our own deficient initiative, that

---

[8] Cf. *Sum. theol.*, I, 63, 1.

thing called nothing (or by nihilating). But if we have not budged, if we have done nothing, that is to say, if we have introduced no nothingness and no *non;* if we allow free passage to these influxes of being, then (and by virtue of the first design of God) the shatterable divine activations fructify by themselves into the unshatterable divine activation. This unshatterable divine activation is none other than the decisive *fiat,* received in us. By Its *fiat* the transcendent Cause makes that to happen which It wills. By virtue of that unshatterable divine activation, our will, this time, unfailingly exercises its liberty in the line of good, produces the good act (vitally consonant with the rule or the *thou shouldst*) towards which tended not only all the activations to good received by the will, but also everything that is good in the will's own inner dynamism, as well as in the fundamental aspiration of its nature.[9] This good act

[9] In as much as the metaphysical substructure here presented may be of some interest to theologians, perhaps it will not be fruitless to define its significance more precisely.

God, the sole agent (other than itself) by which the will can be moved, being the First Cause of all the good produced by created liberty, and His causality not being frustrable, it is clear that no good act, dependent in any way upon the freedom of the will, can come into existence without an unshatterable divine motion. But created liberty being by nature a fallible liberty, we see also that the unshatterable transcendent impetus must normally be preceded by a shatterable transcendent impetus (not to speak of activations of all sorts which pass through creatures,—exhortations, good examples, etc., which we classify, also, as shatterable activations); and this shatterable impetus (which is like a streak of the vivifying radiance in which the created will is immersed) fructifies of itself (when it is not shattered by free nihilating) in the unshatterable motion to which it is ordained and towards which it tends. Therefore, either it is shattered by the nihilating of the free will, or it fructifies in an unshatterable impetus.

was willed by God; He was the first to will it; and
He moved the will to produce it freely under an unshatterable activation. As I remarked above, the first
initiative of this act comes entirely from God and

The shatterable and the unshatterable impetus which
activate either fallibly or infallibly any determined act, differ
by their moral finality from the general motion by which
divine causality universally activates beings, and particularly the physical dynamism of the will.

From the very fact that it is decisive and unconditioned,
the unshatterable transcendent impetus is specifically different from the tendential and shatterable transcendent impetus which precedes it (precedes, at least, according to
the priority of nature). Now if, in the very instant when
its dynamism passes into exercise, the free will has not
nihilated under the influx of the shatterable impetus, at that
very instant, the latter gives way to the unshatterable impetus in which it fructifies and in which, activated by the
unshatterable impetus, the free will projects into existence
something morally good. According to this metaphysical
analysis, the distinction between shatterable and unshatterable impetus concerns all the phases of the dynamism of the
free will, which can produce nothing good except under
the influx of an unshatterable impetus.

In the light of what has just been said it is clear that, if
we consider what is most important in this dynamism,
namely, the act itself of free choice or *election*, we can give
the name of shatterable impetus to everything that prepares
the way for it, including the good acts which, while arising
out of free will, are not yet election (for example, everything good that falls within the *deliberation* which precedes
election). We will then reserve the name of 'unshatterable
impetus' for that impetus which produces the good election.

What is more, if we consider a given act which is *especially important*, (either because of its difficulty or because
of its decisive rôle in the life and destiny of the subject)
we may call 'shatterable impetus' all that precedes it, including all the good acts of free choice, which built a path
leading to it. In this case we will reserve the name 'unshatterable impetus' for that impetus which causes the production of this especially important good choice of election.

The fact remains that, just as nothing in the physical activity of creatures passes into act without the general motion of God, so no morally good act is produced by the free

from creative Liberty, exactly as the second initiative comes entirely from created liberty. The least good act of created liberty is first of all willed by God and it is entirely caused by Him as first cause.

---

will without an unshatterable divine impetus. Besides, we see also that shatterable impetus, from the fact that either it is shattered by free nihilating or it makes way for unshatterable impetus, can never by itself give the *to-do* or the *to-act*, but only the *to-be-able* to do, the proximate power to do the good act.

And yet, being divine motion or activation, it cannot fail to produce an effect in the creature that receives it; and it cannot fail to produce it infallibly (which is nothing else than to say that God really acts upon His creature). But what is this effect immediately produced in the creature by the shatterable impetus? According to a currently approved theological opinion, it is a certain morally good *act* in regard to which the divine activation is efficacious and unshatterable and which gives the *to-act* and the *to-do*, while at the same time it remains merely a sufficient, or shatterable impetus (giving only the *to-be-able* to do) in respect of another moral act, which is higher and ulterior. Thus a grace or an impetus efficacious with regard to a certain direct term (attrition, for example) will be merely sufficient with regard to an ulterior term (say, conversion). And if this merely sufficient grace with regard to conversion be not sterilised by failure in the created existent (which itself supposes a permissive decree of God) it will make way for an efficacious grace with regard to conversion, but one which in its turn will be merely sufficient with regard to another ulterior term (say, perseverance).

In the perspective of our analyses we have to look upon these things differently. The immediate effect (infallibly produced in the creature) of what we call shatterable impetus is not a morally good *act*, but the movement itself, the tendential actuation (impetus as received) of which that act is the final term. And, as we shall attempt to explain below, this *entitas vialis* which traverses the created will may be frustrated (by free nihilating) of its proximate term —frustrated at least in the order of specification (consideration of the rule)—and consequently of its final term (the morally good act to be produced). Thus the shatterable impulse is conceived as giving (dynamically) the ability to act (for moral good), but as not, in any respect, giving the

I do not deny (but this lies outside the purely metaphysical considerations within which I intend to remain) that God can, if He so wills, transport a created existent at one stroke to the performing of a

---

moral *to-act* and *to-do*. And it is conceived as shatterable in relation to the good act itself to be produced by free will. Further it is conceived as ordained of itself, not precisely to the act to be produced by the created will, but rather to the unshatterable impetus itself which will cause that act to be produced and for which the shatterable impetus, if it was not shattered by free nihilating, will make way, as the flower makes way for the fruit, the seed sown in the earth for the wheat, the betrothal for the consummated union. Thus we would conceive a shatterable impetus to attrition which, if it be not shattered by free nihilating, fructifies and vanishes into the unshatterable impetus by virtue of which is produced the act of attrition, and which is followed by a shatterable impetus to conversion, which in its turn, if it be not shattered, will make way for an unshatterable impetus by virtue of which the act of conversion will be produced and which will be succeeded by a shatterable impetus to perseverance, and so on.

In any case it is in this way, namely, as shatterable in relation to the morally good act itself to be produced by free will, that we must conceive the shatterable impetus envisaged in our analysis of the act of freedom. Keeping in mind the *two moments* distinguished by St. Thomas in the genesis of the evil act, this is how the explanation of this essential point appears to us in the present state of our reflections.

The shatterable impetus tends of itself towards a *final term* which will take place at the *second moment* (with which we enter into the order of moral good and evil) and which will be the morally good act to be produced under consideration of the rule. And it tends of itself towards a *direct or proximate term* which will take place at the first moment (where we are still in the merely physical order) and which will be the free application of the intellect to the consideration of the rule (without the act of option being as yet produced).

The effect that the shatterable impetus produces (infallibly) in the created will is tendential actuation, the movement or impulse which traverses the will and which has as its direct and proximate term, as I have just said,

good free act by an unshatterable or infallibly efficacious activation or motion. This is a question of His
free predilections and of the price paid for souls in
the communion of the saints. How far His own wis-

---

the action by which the will moves the intellect to consider
the rule at this first moment (where there is still neither
moral good nor moral evil). Each time that a first agent
or principal agent moves a second agent or instrument, the
latter is traversed by an *entitas vialis* like this, i.e., a tran-
sient and tendential actuation of this sort. But in the
unique case where the second agent in question is the
freedom of the will, and where that second agent can
nihilate, on its own initiative and as a nihilating first cause,
this *entitas vialis* can be frustrated in regard to the direct
term towards which it tends, at least as to the specification
which it connotes, if not as to the exercise which it connotes. Thus the clay of the free will freely fails or fissures
in the hands of the potter.

If the shatterable impetus is shattered by free nihilating,
there is, *at this first moment* (where we are still in the
physical, not moral, order) a non-consideration of the rule.
The shatterable impetus is thus frustrated in regard to its
direct or proximate term, as I have said, in the order of
specification. But in the order of exercise it nevertheless
reaches a term. The only term it reaches is the application
of the intellect by the will to consider something or other—
but not the rule. The activation towards the consideration
of the rule has been freely nihilated. The will, thus de-
flected by free nihilating, causes the intellect to regard
something other than the rule, some apparent good which
lures the desire. *In the second moment* there will be, on
God's side, permission for the effectuation of evil at the
same time as general impetus, particularly to the physical
execution of the evil act. From the side of the created
will, there will be the positing of a deformed free act, deprived of consideration of the rule.

If *at the first moment* (still merely physical) the shatterable impetus is not shattered by free nihilating, at that
same moment it reaches, as regards both specification and
exercise, its direct or proximate term (consideration of the
rule, though still without act of option). It reaches this
of itself and without the least contribution made on its sole
initiative by the created agent, which the impetus besieges
from all sides and which owes to that impetus all the action

dom binds His power, and how far the rule decided by His love binds its impulse to effusion, is the mystery of mysteries. The fact remains that in the order of nature the unshatterable activation is preceded by shatterable activations, as the term in which the latter fructify of themselves when the nihilating of the created liberty has not rendered them sterile.

But what it is important to set forth here with unmistakable clarity is that the created existent contributes nothing of its own, does nothing, adds nothing, gives nothing—not the shadow of an action or of a determination coming from it—which would make of the shatterable impetus an unshatterable impetus or an impetus that comes to grips with ex-

---

that lies within it (not as yet moral). And *at the second moment* (with which we enter into the moral order) it will fructify of itself by reason of its intrinsic ordination, and will vanish into the unshatterable impetus by virtue of which the rule will be efficaciously considered in the very act of option. The final term towards which the shatterable impetus was tending—the morally good act to be produced by the free will—will by produced not by the shatterable impetus itself but by something better than it, something to which it was ordained as the flower to the fruit.

From the moment we understand that if the shatterable impetus is not shattered by the free nihilating of the creature, then it reaches of itself its proximate term, in order to give way to an unshatterable impetus specifically distinct from itself, in which it fructifies of itself and by which the morally good *to-act* is given; from the moment we understand that the *non-nihilating*, which conditions the fructification of the shatterable impetus in unshatterable impetus, does absolutely not imply the slightest contribution made by the creature to the divine motion—from this moment we have beyond question exorcised every shadow of Molinism.

These explanations may perhaps help to display how the metaphysical notions of shatterable and unshatterable impetus can serve as foundation for the theological notions of sufficient and efficacious grace, and furnish from below a contribution to the rational clarification of those notions.

istence. Not to nihilate under the divine activation, not to sterilise that impetus, not to have the initiative of making the thing we call nothing, does not mean taking the initiative, or the demi-initiative, or the smallest fraction of the initiative of an act; it does not mean acting on one's own to complete, in any way whatever, the divine activation. It means not stirring under its touch, but allowing it free passage, allowing it to bear its fruit (the unshatterable activation) by virtue of which the will (which did not nihilate in the first instance) will act (will look at the rule efficaciously) in the very exercise of its domination over its motives, and will burst forth freely in a good option and a good act.[10] It will then be all

[10] To allow the shatterable impetus free passage is to let it fructify of itself and disappear into the unshatterable impetus by virtue of which the good act is produced, namely the rule efficaciously regarded in the very act of option.

It is proper to remark here that if 'not to nihilate' and 'to consider the rule' come practically to the same thing, nevertheless there is, formally, a clear distinction between the two, and the first formality is the condition of the second. 'Not to nihilate' relates to the *first* initiative which the creature can take *and does not take*. 'Not to nihilate' signifies that the creature does *nothing* through its own movement. Nothing emanates from it as first cause. It is not its power as (nihilating) first cause which is exercised in order to not-nihilate! That power purely and simply is *not* exercised. From the side of the creature, as first initiative, there is *nothing*.

Contrariwise, 'to consider the rule' relates to the *second* initiative which the creature takes under the motion of the first divine initiative (which anticipates it by the shatterable impetus, and which is exercised in unshatterable impetus only if the creature has not nihilated). 'To consider the rule' signifies either—at the moment preceding the act of option—that the creature exercises an action (which is not yet moral) under the activation of the shatterable impetus itself attaining its direct term, without there being at the moment in question (contrary to what happens in the case of the evil act) any ontological pre-condition to the moral

the more aided by God, for there is no aid stronger
than that which possesses a decidedly existential
value, which decidedly and efficaciously causes an
act freely posited to come into existence—an act sur-
rounded on all sides with being and with goodness.
One man may have received shatterable motions or
activations of a higher sort than those received by
another. If one renders them sterile by freely nihil-

---

act, which would be due to the first created initiative; or—
at the moment when the act of option takes place—that the
creature acts (morally) under the unshatterable impetus for
which way was made by the shatterable motion which was
not shattered. Everything in the regard which is freely
turned upon the rule comes from God as first cause, and
everything comes from the creature as second cause, without there being, on the side of the creature, any other condition than that of having done *nothing* by its first initiative
as nihilating first cause.

We are far from being able to say that the least contribution made by the created existent renders the shatterable
impetus unshatterable. On the contrary, it is the shatterable impetus which of itself makes way for the unshatterable impetus and fructifies in it by the sole fact that the
created existent did *nothing* of itself alone. For the shatterable impetus, by its very nature, tended to the unshatterable
impetus and was ordered to it from its very origin. 'Not to
nihilate' adds absolutely nothing to the divine motion. The
created existent which nihilates, 'discerns itself' for the evil
and the failure, or destines itself to this end; because it
takes the first initiative of nihilating. He who does not
nihilate does not destine himself to the possession of God,
because he takes no first initiative of being or of goodness,
and because he does *nothing* on his first initiative, contributes *nothing* by himself alone. It is the divine will
which, in all eternity, destines him to the possession of
God *ante praevisa merita*, by a primordial but conditional
ordination which extends to all men without exception. If,
precisely, he does *nothing* on his first initiative (which implies neither the least act nor the least merit) that primordial ordination is confirmed by the definitive ordination in
which he is unconditionally marked for final accomplishment.

'Deus omnipotens *omnes homines* sine exceptione *vult*

ating, while the other does not render sterile those
which he received, and which fructify of themselves
in unshatterable activation, that other will have been
more greatly loved. He will have been loved to the
degree which counts above all else, the degree of
the communication or effusion of goodness in the exercise of the existence and effectuation of the act.

Transposing for our purposes, and into our wholly
metaphysical perspective, a classical distinction of
theology,[11] we shall give the name of primordial or
original will to the will of God considered without
regard to particular conditions or circumstances—
what we may also call His 'naked' will. This will is

---

salvos fieri (I Timothy II, 4) licet non omnes salventur.
Quod autem quidam salvantur, salvantis est donum; quod
autem quidem pereunt, pereuntium est meritum.' Conc.
Carisiacum, Denziger-Bannwart-Umberg, Enchiridion Sym-
bolorum, Freiburg im B., 1947, 318.

'Deus namque sua gratia semel justificatos *non deserit,
nisi ab eis prius deseratur* (S. Aug., *De nat. et gratia, c. 26*,
N. 29. P.L. 44, 261).' Conc. Tridentinum, Denziger-Bannwart-Umberg, *op. cit.*, 804.

[11] Cf. St. John Damascene, *De fide Orthodoxa*, Lib. II,
Cap. 29, P.G. 94, 967-970; St. Thomas Aquinas, *De Veritate*,
23, 2 and 3; John of St. Thomas (*Cursus Theologicus* [Vivès
ed.] Tome III, Quaest. XIX, Disp. 5, Art. 8, pp. 481-500;
[Solesmes ed.] Tome III, In quaest. XIX Iae P. Disp. 25,
Art 8, pp. 260-278.) When theologians distinguish in
God between the antecedent will and the consequent
will, they do not mean that two different acts of
will are present in God, but they refer to a simple and
unique will in pure act which has as its *term* either something willed as primordially or originally, and in a manner
that will not be infallibly followed by effect, or something
willed as definitively and in a manner which will be infallibly followed by effect. This is translated, in our human
manner of conception, by the virtual distinction between
will called antecedent and will called consequent (or, in
our metaphysical vocabulary, between will called primordial
and will called definitive).

not a velleity, it is a true and active will which projects into the universality of existents the being and
goodness that penetrate them and the flux of incita-
tions, motions, and activations that make them tend
towards their fulfilment and towards the common
good of creation. By this primordial will, the creative
Love wills that all free existents attain to their supra-temporal end.[12] It wills this independently of every consideration of the good or meritorious acts they
may perform, wills it out of pure generosity. But it
wills it according to the mode of their own fallible
freedom, that is to say, according to shatterable motions or activations. And if the will that we shall call
'circumstanced,' and which is the will of God considered as taking account of particular conditions
and circumstances (we may also call it His 'definitive' will), allows free existents to miss their supra-
temporal end, what can be the circumstance of
which the creative Love then takes account, unless
it be that of the nihilating by which, in the course
of their existence, and especially at the last instant
of their existence, their freedom evades His influx
and renders the divine activation sterile? Suppose
that this initiative of nihilation do not take place on
the part of the free existent; then, as concerns that
free existent, the circumstanced will purely and
simply confirms, in unconditionally and unfailingly
efficacious fashion, the primordial will which, in
willing the final good of all, itself ordained it (con-
ditionally) to this good. Free existents which attain
their ultimate end attain it only because God willed
it, prior to every consideration of their good and
meritorious acts, by His primordial will confirmed

[12] Cf. I Timothy II, 4: 'Deus omnes homines vult salvos
fieri et ad agnitionem veritatis venire.'

(as I have just said) by His definitive will. The free existents who miss their ultimate end do so only because they have willed to miss it and have freely evaded that which was ordained by the primordial will. God permits this on account of the initiative of nihilating by which their freedom, especially at the last instant of their lives, rendered the divine activation sterile and thereupon flung them into evil. These, St. Thomas used to say, are the fore-known (*praesciti*); the others are the predestined. And all this is established from all eternity because every moment of time is present to the divine eternity and to the eternal will and eternal vision of God.

I am aware that by employing two of St. Thomas's words I have moved into a realm that I had proscribed for myself. I am aware that the ultimate end of free existents being in fact a supernatural end, the vision of God Himself, I should write 'salvation' where I have written attainment of the supra-temporal end, 'predestination' where I have written ordainment to the final good confirmed by the definitive will, 'antecedent will and consequent will' where I have written primordial will and definitive will, 'sufficient grace and efficacious grace' where I have written shatterable impetus and unshatterable impetus. I am aware that vast theological problems in which faith is involved arise and complicate the simple views of reason which I have advanced under a merely metaphysical aspect.[13]

[13] We are not presently concerned with these problems. We should like, however, to make two observations. First, the domain of grace is that of the sovereign liberty and the sovereign transcendence of the *Deus excelsus, terribilis*, Who does injustice to none by giving to one more than He gives (also gratuitously) to another, and Who, in governing created liberties in their progress here below, can use,

But I believe that the purely philosophical consideration of the principles of the natural order involved in the problem of the destiny of free existents, which I have attempted to grapple with, can lead to a sort of rational plan which would not be destroyed but rather exalted by passing to the higher and deeper and more complex views of theology.

The Divine Science

31. Sixth consideration: *Divine knowledge of the free acts of the created existent.* We must never lose sight of the fact that the divine understanding or divine science, the pure Act of knowledge which is God Himself and His pure Act of existing, is totally and absolutely independent of things. The divine understanding is its own object. Created beings are not

---

when He pleases, exceptional ways which exceed the ordinary governance required by nature—for example, by giving at one stroke to some among them (I think of Paul on the road to Damascus) an unshatterable impetus to conversion. Secondly, as concerns the primordial mystery of predestination, and the application which a theologian could make of the metaphysical presuppositions here indicated, we should like to observe that these metaphysical presuppositions are in strict accord with what sacred tradition teaches concerning this mystery. The created existents which, according to the conception put forth by us, are ordained in all eternity to eternal life, *ante praevisa merita,* by the primordial or 'antecedent' will confirmed by the definitive or 'consequent' will (from the moment they did *not* take the initiative of nihilating at the critical juncture) were by the definitive or 'consequent' will *inscribed in the book of life before the world was created.* We must say of them what St. Paul says: 'quos praedestinavit, hos et vocavit, et quos vocavit, hos et justificavit: quos autem justificavit, illos et glorificavit.' (Romans VIII, 30).

its object.[14] They do not in any way specify or determine it; with regard to it they are merely a *terminus materialiter attactus*,[15] a field that is *gratuitously permeated* by way of excess and surplus goodness. They change, are born, and perish; but the knowledge or understanding which God has of them does not change. This divine science knows all things. But even if God had not created anything, if there were no things, God's knowledge or science itself would remain perfectly unchanged; because it is God Who is its object. He fills and saturates it. Imagine a poet completely enraptured in the absolute knowledge of his soul. Whether or not his knowledge superabound in song, the words he utters in his poetry or does not utter at all do not alter that knowledge itself. The beings he creates in his poetry are attained and permeated, transpermeated, by his knowledge as by a gratuitous super-effluence. Indeed, they are made by that knowledge. They neither touch nor change that subsistent flash of self-knowledge. God knows and loves all existents. They do not impinge upon His knowledge and His love after the manner of specifying objects. In the act by which He knows Himself and loves His own goodness, God embraces all existents as *effects* flowing from the infinite gratuitousness in which that act superabounds.[16]

---

[14] In the proper meaning of the term object, namely, the specifying term of knowledge. Cf. St. Thomas, *In Metaph.*, XII, 11, Cathala ed., pp. 2614-2616 in connection with the famous text of Aristotle, *Met.*, XII, 9, 1074b, 29-35.

[15] "Nude terminativum et materiale objectum." John of St. Thomas, *Curs. theol.*, (Vivès ed.) Tome II, Quaest. XIV, *Disp.* 17, A. 2, p. 464; (Solesmes ed.) Tome II, In Quaest. XIV Iae P. *Disp.* 17, Art. 2, p. 361.

[16] Cf. John of St. Thomas, *Cursus Theologicus* (Vivès ed.), Tome III, Quaest. XIX, Disp. 4, Art. 3, p. 238;

God knows all things in Himself or in His essence, in the uncreated light, which is His own infinite intelligibility and which is infinitely more limpid and richer than the intelligibility of things.

In His essence He knows possibles by a necessary knowledge, a knowledge as necessary as that which He has of Himself. According to our human way of conceiving, and the virtual distinctions to which we are forced to have recourse, it must be said that neither His will nor His liberty intervenes in that knowledge. For this reason it is called the 'science of simple intelligence.'

Existents also are known to Him in His essence. They are known, as I have already remarked, as gratuitous surplus, and by a creative knowledge in which will and liberty are linked with intellect, a knowledge which freely makes *known,* as it freely makes *existent* that which it creates. Here all contingency is on the side of the term of this creative knowledge. This is what is called the 'science of vision,' because it passes beyond simple intellection of essences and bears upon existence and the existent.

I have said that God knows all things in His essence. I have not said, God forbid! that in His essence, He knows images resembling things but not things themselves. Such a conception would simply make of the divine essence a mosaic of portraits of the finite. In the intelligibility in pure act of the infinite essence, which is at one His own act of existing and the object of His knowledge, God knows the multitude of finite beings as so many participations in that essence. He passes through the infinite to reach the finite. But He reaches the finite itself and

(Solesmes ed.) Tome III, In Quaest. XIX Iae P. Disp. 24, Art. 3, p. 77.

does so in a necessarily exhaustive understanding since it is that very act of knowing which makes things be.

In knowing His essence God knows all possibles in all the recesses of their intelligibility. In knowing His essence and His will (by which He necessarily wills His own goodness and freely wills things) He knows all existents in all the recesses of their being. The 'science of vision' reaches the existent in the very exercise of existence. It holds and trans-permeates all created existents because it creates all that is in them and because it is by knowing them that it creates them. In the very act by which God's 'science of vision' gratuitously sets up created existents as terms of the act by which He knows Himself, or as things *known* to Him (by the excess of His own self-knowledge), in that very act the 'science of vision' freely makes them terms of the creative action and constitutes them beings in their own existence. It possesses the world of existence and of the existent, of subjects and of subjectivities, from within; it sees contingent existence because it causes it, and because, by making it *known,* it makes it *be.*

The 'science of vision' likewise reaches the freedom of the created existent in the very exercise of its free choice. We know that the free act is absolutely unforeseeable. But the 'science of vision' does not 'foresee' the free act but grasps it eternally in its very presentness, in the very instant in which it is produced.

All that is, is known to God because He causes it. Such is the case of the free act of the created existent. When that act is good, it is known to God because all that is in it derives from the divine super-causality as from its first transcendent cause.

But how does God's science know the evil of the free will, the evil which makes the free act evil? On this point, St. Thomas has two principles which deserve to be meditated upon. First, *God is absolutely not a cause of moral evil,*[17] *not in any respect whatsoever.* Here, therefore, is something that God knows without having caused it (something which is not a thing but a privation). Secondly, *there is no idea of evil in the divine intellect,* because the divine idea signifies a way in which the divine essence can be participated and is therefore of itself the source of intelligibility or the cause of being.[18] The purity of God, the innocence of God, is such that He has the idea only of good, He has not the idea of evil. It is we who have that idea. God knows evil for what it is: a privation, a nihilating which wounds being; and He knows it at the point where it occurs—in the being that it wounds or in the good that it defaces.

[17] This principle is not peculiar to St. Thomas; it is essential to the Catholic faith. St. Thomas points out that it is found in St. Augustine: 'Sed contra est quod dicit Augustinius in libro Octog. trium Quaest. quod Deus non est auctor mali, quia non est causa tendendi ad *non esse.*' The passage referred to reads as follows: Quisquis omnium quae sunt auctor est et ad cujus bonitatem id tantum pertinet ut sit omne quod est non esse ad eum pertinere nullo pacto potest. Omne autem quod deficit, ab eo quod est esse deficit et tendit in non esse. Esse autem et in nullo deficere bonum est, et malum est deficere. At ille ad quem non esse non pertinet non est causa deficiendi, i.e., tendendi ad non esse; quia, ut ita dicam, essendi causa est. (St. Augustine, De Diversis Quaestionibus Octoginta tres. Qu. 21, P.L. 40. 16). 'Deus est auctor mali quod est poena, non autem mali quod est culpa,' *Sum. theol.,* I, 49, 2, c. 'Deus non potest esse causa peccati,' *Ibid.,* 63, 5, c. 'Deus *nullo modo* est causa peccati nec directe nec indirecte.' I-II, 79, 1, c.

[18] 'Malum non habet in Deo ideam, neque secundum quod idea est exemplar, neque secundum quod est ratio.' *Sum. theol.,* I, 15, 2, *ad* 1.

The evil of the free act has as its first cause (nihilating, not efficient, cause) not God but the free will of the created existent. How, then, could it be known by a divine volition (even permissive) which would precede its engendering by the creature as the divine volition of the good act precedes that act? There are two divine permissions without which evil would never reach existence. One is the permission of the *possibility* of evil, enveloped in advance in the frustrability of what we have called the shatterable divine impetus which created liberty, if it so wills, is able to render sterile. The other is the permission for the *effectuation* of evil,[19] once created liberty has already nihilated in fact, but without having as yet acted (in that moment of non-consideration of the rule which precedes the evil option). But that moment itself, when the creature takes the initiative of making the thing called nothing and thereby asks, so to say, permission to do evil—that moment precedes the permission given it, consequently it is not known in that permission, i.e., in the non-will to apply a remedy to that nihilating. It can be known only in the actually deficient or nihilating free will.

How? Is it not in His essence that God knows things? I answer that He knows in Himself alone all that which is causable or caused by Him, though it be only by accident (like the evil of nature[20]). But what is not causable nor caused by Him, that of which He is absolutely not the cause, like the evil

[19] Here, in the permission for the *effectuation* of evil, is situated the notion of permissive decree (including permission that the general motion which activates the whole physical order be not withheld from the physical content of the evil act).

[20] Cf. *Sum. theol.*, I, 49, 2.

of the free act and like the free nihilating which is
its precondition, these God does not know in the divine essence considered alone, but in the divine essence in as much as created existents are seen
therein, and in as much as in *them* is seen that nihilating and privation of which their freedom is the
first cause. In other terms, He knows that nihilating
and that privation *in* the created existents whom He
knows *in* His essence. It is in this sense that I said
that the 'non-consideration of the rule' which precedes the evil option (that nihilating whose importance is crucial for the present discussion because
it is a pure non-being due solely to the freedom of
the existent) is known to God in the actually deficient or nihilating will.[21]

The knowledge of God is not determined or speci-
fied by anything other than God. It knows ('science
of simple intelligence') possible creatures in God
alone; I mean in the divine essence taken as such.
Their possibility cannot be abolished any more than
the divine essence itself of which they are participations eternally and necessarily seen by the understanding which God possesses of Himself. And it
knows ('science of vision') created existents and all
the being and liberty they possess, in God alone; I
mean in the divine essence taken not only as the
ground of all possibles but as enveloping the divine
will which freely determines certain among them to
exist in an existence which is not that of God. And
finally the divine science knows the fissure of non-
being or the nihilating (the vacuum, the pure absence, the moment of non-consideration of the rule,

[21] Cf. J. Maritain, *Frontières de la poésie* ('La Clef des
Chants'), pp. 189-192. Eng. trans., *Art and Poetry*, N. Y.,
1943, pp. 84-86.

which has its origin only in the liberty of created existence) in the actually nihilating will of created existents known in God—that is, in the divine essence *conjointly* with the gratuitous surplus embraced by it—or, to put it in another way, in the created existents whom the science of God knows in the divine essence and knows exhaustively because creatively; whom it holds entirely in its hand, down to the last cranny and the least quiverings of their subjectivity and their activity.

It knows this pure absence without having caused it, and yet without having received anything from the creature. How, indeed, could a bit of non-being determine or specify anything at all? *A fortiori* it could not determine or specify pure Act, whose touch affects all things but which is affected by none. The divine science knows this absence as a *terminus materialiter attactus*. And this 'terminus' is not a being. It is the vacuum or negation, the lacuna actually produced in the being which the 'science of vision' wholly embraces, and which itself is formed like clay in the hands of the potter by God's knowledge, but does not form or cause that knowledge. And because God knows, in the created existent whom He knows in His essence, this fissure of nothingness of which the freedom of the created existent is the first cause, God (if He does not will to remedy it) does not prevent—that is, He permits the evil to work itself out in the free act of which that fissure is the precondition.

That evil itself, which is not a mere lacuna or pure absence, but is a privation, is effected in the free act. It makes of that act something, in the moral line, purely and simply evil; but, in so far as the act contains being and energy, it retains metaphysical goodness and depends to that extent upon divine causality. However, in so far as it is moral evil, God is in no wise its cause. We must therefore say of it what we said of the moment of nihilating which precedes it: God knows it in the created existent whom He knows in the divine essence. That privation, a moral evil which wounds the act of the creature, is known to God without being caused by Him, by the fact that in the divine essence created existents are *seen*, moral evil is known in them, in the panorama of those existents which are embraced by the 'science of vision'—a spectacle which might never have been. He did not invent evil; it is we who invent it. We are its first cause (nihilating, not efficient). It is our creation.

The Eternal Plan

32. Seventh and final consideration: *God's eternal plan and the free existents.* We may now conclude. God's plan is eternal, as is the creative act itself, though it have its effect in time. God's plan is established from all eternity. But eternity is not a kind of divine time which precedes time. It is a limitless instant which indivisibly embraces the whole succession of time. All the moments of that succession are physically present in it. If all things are naked and open to the eyes of God it is because they are seen by His divine 'science of vision' in their presentness. 'To foresee' is an improper word to use when speaking of God. We employ it because we project into His eternity the anteriority (in relation to future events) of the knowledge which *we would have* of those events if *we* knew them *before* they happened.

They are known to Him 'already,' which is to say, always. He sees them as actually taking place at a given temporal instant which is present in His eternity. All things and all events in nature are known to Him at their first coming forth and in the eternal morning of His vision, because they are willed by Him, beyond all time, in the eternal instant with which their whole succession coexists.

But when we deal with the world of freedom, and not only with that of nature, when we deal with free existents, creatures endowed with freedom of choice (a freedom inevitably fallible), we must go still farther. We must say that in a certain fashion those creatures have their part in the very establishment of the eternal plan, not, indeed, by virtue of their power to act (here all they have they hold of God) but by virtue of their power to nihilate, to make the thing that is nothing, where they themselves are first causes. Free existents have their part in the establishment of God's plan, because in establishing that plan, He takes account of their initiatives of nihilating.

The divine plan was always willed. Assuming that God willed it at all, it cannot but be that He willed it *always*.[22] Yet conversely, assuming that He had not willed it, it would necessarily have to be that He had *never* willed it. He freely willed it always, for all its contingency is on the side of *that which* is directed and ordained, not on the side of the act that directs and ordains it. And I say that, since the spectacle of created existents ordained and directed (i.e., the term, or matter, of the divine plan) is essentially and radically contingent; and since this contingency

[22] Cf. *Sum. theol.*, I, 19, 3; *Summa contra Gentiles*, lib. I, cap. 81-83.

in no way affects the divine plan itself or the divine act that established it, there is nothing to prevent the free nihilating of the creature from intervening in this contingency of the spectacle immutably ordained and directed by God. For that nihilating is itself eternally and immutably seen by God, without for that reason introducing a shadow of contingency into His knowledge. And since the spectacle of created beings is ordained and directed from all eternity—not *in advance* (as if eternity were itself in time and the eternal act a thing of the past), but in the eternal *to-day* in which all the successive moments of existence are indivisibly present—since this is so, the effect which ensues from that nihilating is eternally and immutably permitted or non-permitted by God without for this reason introducing a shadow of contingency or of conditioning into His will.[23]

The divine plan is not a scenario prepared in advance, in which free subjects would play parts and act as performers. We must purge our thought of any idea of a play written in advance, at a time prior to time—a play in which time unfolds, and the characters of time read the parts. On the contrary, every-

[23] The will of God is not, like ours, a 'power' or 'faculty' which produces acts: it is pure act. There is in it no act of will susceptible of being conditioned by another act of will, or by any created circumstance. For example, God does not make an act of will to punish a sinning creature, which act would be conditioned by the creature's sin. The eternal act of will by which God wills necessarily His own goodness (which is His being itself) freely *renders* (by a gratuitous surplus) such and such acts or events *willed* or *permitted*. They are, moreover, rendered *willed* or *permitted* as ordained to a given end, or depending upon certain circumstances and certain conditions. In this, however, all the contingency and all the conditioning is on the side of the term.

thing is improvised, under the eternal and immutable direction of the almighty Stage Manager. The divine plan is the ordination of the infinite multiplicity of things, and of their becoming, by the absolutely simple gaze of the creative knowledge and the will of God. It is eternal and immutable, but it could have been otherwise (since it could not have been had there not been things). *Once fixed* from all eternity, once *assumed* as fixed in such and such a way from all eternity, it is immutable. And it is by virtue of the eternal presence of time in eternity (even before time was), by virtue of the embrace, by the eternal instant, of history in the making (perpetually fresh in its newness and indeed—as regards free acts—in its unforeseeability) that the divine plan is immutably fixed in heaven from all eternity, directing history towards the ends willed by God and disposing towards those ends all the actors in the drama and all the good God causes in them, while taking advantage, on behalf of those ends, of the evil itself of which they are the nihilating first cause and which God permits without having caused it.

By reason of this free nihilating, the creature has a portion of first initiative in the drama. Unless the free existent has received at one stroke an unshatterable impetus to good, it depends solely upon him whether he will or will not take the initiative of nihilating or of non-consideration of the rule, under the motions and activations which bear him towards good. Will he or will he not nihilate under the hand of the potter? As concerns his good or evil act, and the repercussions it may have upon what follows in the drama, it is at that instant in time, known from all eternity, that the immutable plan is simultaneously established from all eternity. Let us suppose that the free creature has not, in that instant, the initiative of the thing that is nothing. The initiative of nihilating not being seen (from all eternity) in the free existent by the 'science of vision,' from all eternity, the primordial will of God (which willed the good act of this creature in the direction of the particular end towards which it ordained him) is confirmed by the definitive or circumstanced will. Thus from all eternity the accomplishment of this good act by this creature is immutably fixed in the eternal plan. Let us suppose, on the contrary, that at that instant the free creature has the initiative of the thing that is nothing. Then, this is seen from all eternity in the free existent by the 'science of vision'; and from all eternity God's definitive or circumstanced will (if it does not will to prevent the natural effect of this nihilating) permits the evil act of which this creature has the first initiative; and from all eternity the permission of this evil act, ordained to a better good (itself willed either determinately or indeterminately),[24] is immutably fixed in the eternal plan. Thus we can conceive, by the aid of the mo-

[24] There is nothing that is willed indeterminately, if we consider the eternal will and the *entire* procession of events in time with all the free acts contained therein. But in relation to a *given moment* in history and in time, where a given event is willed or permitted, I understand by 'good willed indeterminately' a good willed as to be attained, by modes, ways, and determinations which, *considering that moment in time* and taking account of the free nihilations which can still intervene and bring about other divine permissions, are not yet fixed. All is eternally fixed in the eternal plan, where there is no succession and which embraces every time. But we cannot imagine any idea of this eternal plan and the ordinations it includes except by introducing the distinctions of reason and the moments of reason required by our human mode of conceiving.

ments of reason which our human mode of conceiving is forced to distinguish in the divine will, that the variegated drama of history and humanity, with its infinite interweavings, is immutably fixed from all eternity by the perfectly and infinitely simple dominating act of divine knowledge and free will, account being taken of all free existents and of all the free nihilations of which these existents have or have not the initiative, throughout the whole succession of time whose every moment is present in eternity. Let no one say that man alters the eternal plan! That would be an absurdity. Man does not alter it. He enters into its very composition and its eternal fixity by his power of saying, No!

To tell the truth, I do not see how things could be conceived otherwise. Suppose that the eternal plan were a scenario prepared in advance. Suppose that in that scenario it was written that Brutus was to assassinate Caesar.[25] Then, when Brutus steps forth upon the stage of the world, either the Stage Manager will leave him truly free to have or not have the first initiative of sin, in which case Brutus might not murder Caesar and might thus frustrate the eternal plan—which is absurd; or else the Stage Manager will arrange in one way or another, with antecedent permissive decrees or supercomprehensions of causes, that Brutus really assassinate Caesar but still commit the murder freely. How then and by what subtleties, can one avoid the conclusion that God had the first initiative of the sin, and, were it

[25] St. Thomas, in the commentary on the *Sentences* (II, dist. 44, 9, 2, a. 2, ad. 5), excuses this sin in Brutus. Dante, meanwhile (*Paradiso* c. 6, v. 74), puts him with Judas in the lowest circle of hell. Here, for the sole purpose of the argument, we adopt Dante's view and assume that Brutus was a criminal.

merely by slackening His hand, caused the creature to fall into it?

It was Brutus who had the first initiative of the free nihilating by which, God permitting, the decision of murder entered into his will and into the history of the world. If, at that instant in time, eternally present in the eternal instant, he had not had that initiative of nihilating, the immutable plan would have fixed things in another way from all eternity. Caesar's fall would have been led up to by other ways, as would also the accomplishment of God's designs with regard to Rome and to the world to which that fall was related and for which it was willed.

I have said that in God there is no idea of evil. He invented Behemoth and Leviathan, and all the terrifying forms which people nature and the world of life—the ferocious fishes, the destroying insects. He did not invent moral evil and sin. It was not He who had the idea of all the defilements and abominations and contempts that are spat into His Face; the betrayals, lecheries, cruelties, cowardices, bestial wickednesses, refined perversions, depravities of mind which it is given to His creatures to contemplate. Those were born solely of nihilation by human liberty. They came forth from that abyss. God permits them as a creation of our power to make the thing which is nothing.

He permits them because He is strong enough, as St. Augustine says, to turn all the evil we choose to introduce into the world, into a greater good—hidden in the mystery of transcendence and such that nothing in nature allows us to conjecture what it may consist in. The man of faith, who is to have a suspicion of the greatness of that good, and marvel at it, measures the greatness of the evil for which such a good will supercompensate.

Our misfortune is precisely that there is no scenario written by God in advance (it would be less sinister); and that the ill-omened element of the drama comes from created existents, ourselves; and from the fact that God plays fair. Since the evil of the free act is our creation, it is in letting our monsters proliferate to the very end, and allowing the infinite resources of our power of nihilating to develop all forms of degradation and corruption of being, that divine liberty manifests the sublimity of its omnipotence by drawing *from that itself* the higher good which God designs, not for Himself but for us.[26] Meanwhile, despite all the energies of goodness at work in man, nature, and history, which cause them to advance by rising above their ruins, 'the whole world is seated in wickedness'[27] and the terrible, the incorruptible, divine fair play leaves us to flounder in the mire. Such at least is the way in which it is allowable for a philosopher to look upon the order of nature. Fortunately, there is also the order of grace, and the virtue of the blood of Christ, the sufferings and prayers of the saints, and the hidden operations of mercy. All these, without infringing the laws of divine fair play, introduce into the most secret recesses of the plot factors which transfigure it. They manifest the heavenly ordering according to which souls are deputed to eternal life, bodies to resurrection, and the wickedness of the free creatures becomes the price paid for glory. On this very earth, they make love prevail over sin (if,

[26] *Deus gloriam suam quaerit non propter se, sed propter nos.* St. Thomas Aquinas, *Sum. theol.*, II-II, 132, 1, *ad* 1.

[27] *Mundus totus in maligno positus est.* I John V, 19.

at least, we have eyes to see); and they come invisibly to help each one to reach the hereafter even while the sad, ordinary laws and the miseries of the herebefore are at work upon all. For those who serve God they cause all things to cooperate in goodness, and to cover with His wings those who have given all to Him. They strengthen the springs and the resources of nature by offering, in spite of everything, their mercy; by bringing, in spite of everything, their succour; by giving, in spite of everything, some respite to peoples and to nations; and, in spite of everything, by guiding history towards its accomplishment. A more than human grandeur is dissembled in our creeping destinies. A sense is given to our wretched condition; and this is probably what matters most to us. It remains a wretched condition —but the existent who vegetates in it is cut out to become God by participation.

Chapter Five

ECCE IN PACE

*From Existential Existentialism to
Academic Existentialism*

33. In the last essay he left to his friends before being led away and put to death behind the bars of racism, Benjamin Fondane wrote that for Kierkegaard and the 'first existential generation' the nothingness which anguish reveals to man 'is not a nothingness *of* the existent but is a nothingness *in* the existent. It is the crack in the existent: sin, the "swoon of liberty." '[1]

If, as I too believe, such is the genuine and deepest meaning of Kierkegaardian anguish, it must be said that by way of a spiritually crucifying existence, Kierkegaard revealed to modern philosophy a truth which undoubtedly was always known to the saints and was always more or less scrutinised by theologians, but which went far beyond philosophy; a truth which modern philosophy was unable to understand and which has disorganised it.

The nothingness of which I myself am the cause, which ravages my being and causes my God to die; the loud cry that rises from the depths, the terror of

[1] Benjamin Fondane, 'Le Lundi existentiel et le Dimanche de l'histoire,' in *L'Existence*, Paris, 1945, p. 35.

Good Friday, the drama of the *infelix homo*—('but
I am carnal, sold under sin; for that which I work, I
understand not: for I do not that good which I will:
but the evil which I hate, that I do. . . . Unhappy
man that I am; who shall deliver me from the body
of this death?'[2])—Abraham's sacrifice; Job's sores
and his lament, more glorious to God than all the
theodicies; the unanswerable questionings raised by
the existent in the direction of the mystery of the
Castle and the divine ways,—all this irrupted suddenly into modern philosophy, shook its fine confidence, ruffled its serenity. But not for long. Modern philosophy quickly took hold of itself.

Normally and necessarily, according to the laws
inscribed in our being, there are among men and
even in the same man (in whom they can and
ought to coexist on different lines) two attitudes or
rather tensions, two fundamentally different postures
of the mind. The first I shall call the posture of
cause-seeking. This attitude is characterised by a
certain theoretical universality or detachment from
self for the purpose of knowing: the *sapiential* mien
or bearing. This is the attitude of the intellect concerned to know and apprehend being: the bearing
of Minerva, let us say, confronting the cosmos. The
other I shall call the posture of *saving my all*, the
attitude of dramatic singularity or supreme struggle
for the salvation of self, the *imprecatory* mien or
bearing, that of the man who wills his God, or rather
is willed by Him: the bearing of Jacob, say, wrestling
with the Angel.

The first attitude, tension, or posture is essentially
philosophical. It is this that makes the philosopher.

[2] Romans VII, 14-15, 24.

The second is essentially religious. It makes the man
of faith (or one who despairs of God). It is non-sense
to think of making the bearing or posture of Jacob
in the night of his combat with the angel the attitude
of metaphysics, with its special way of coming to
grips with the law of things. It is non-sense to think
of making the bearing or posture of Minerva in her
search for causes the attitude of faith, with its special manner of tackling the dialogue with the God
of faith. We do not philosophise in the posture of
dramatic singularity; we do not save our souls in the
posture of theoretical universality and detachment
from self for the purpose of knowing.

Clearly, the second of these two attitudes, postures, or tensions which I have just distinguished,
the posture of *saving my all,* was that of *existential
existentialism* lived and exercised (*in actu exercito*).
In this very fact lay the grandeur of its testimony,
the power of its shattering strength, and the value
of its intuitions. The existentialism of Kierkegaard,
of Kafka,[3] of Chestov, of Fondane, was an essentially religious irruption and claim, an agony of
faith, the cry of the subjectivity towards its God. It
was at the same time a revelation of the person and
of his anguish in the face of the nothingness which
is non-being *in* the existent, the 'crack *in* the existent.'

But because of the historic circumstances in
which it was born, and particularly because of Hegel
and the implacable fascination of his totalitarianism
of the reason, it was the misfortune of this existentialism to arise and develop *within philosophy.* As it
arose and developed it was inseparable from the

[3] Cf. Max Brod, 'Kierkegaard, Heidegger et Kafka,' in
L'Arche, November, 1946.

philosophy with which it was in merciless conflict, held and gripped by the very philosophy it was seeking to strike to the heart—the principle of non-contradiction. Existential existentialism was thus like a man struggling in the coils of a gigantic reptile. By an astounding mistake, and as the effect of an inevitable illusion, this protest of a faith, caught in a Babylonian captivity, came forth into the world dressed in the livery of Babylon. It was a religious protest *in the guise of a philosophy*—a philosophy directed against the professionals of philosophy; and this was, of course, most comforting. But also (and here an entire tragedy was involved), it was a philosophy *against philosophy*.

Professionals always get their revenge. The game was lost before it began. Existential existentialism was doomed to be the prey of the boa constrictor. Modern philosophy was to adopt it, make it its own, digest it, assimilate it, and, thanks to it, apply restoratives to the old frame of its worn-out concepts. *Philosophical* or *academic existentialism* was bound to come: existentialism as designed (*in actu signato*), as a machine for making ideas, as an apparatus for the fabrication of theses. And indeed the blame should be put on existential existentialism which, except in the case of Kafka, had mistaken itself for a philosophy. The philosophical (I dare not say, *sapiential*) posture was naturally and inevitably to replace the *imprecatory* posture, and with it the agony and the anguish, of the man of faith. Or rather, when current thought went back once more to the philosophical attitude (which is noble and necessary if man venerates the reason by which he lives, but vain and degraded if he flouts it), that agony and that anguish were to be treasured, but because they now became *that which* philosophers talk and dilate upon, not *that which* makes one talk or rave. They were to be retained as new principles upon which systems would be built, and as new themes to be artfully exploited. The cry sent up from the depth of the abyss has become a philosophical theme. Minerva (but what a Minerva!) has carried off Jacob's ladder to her workshop. She is sawing it up into segments of theatre settings and of seats for literary bigwigs.

This fine task was not accomplished without some wear and tear upon Minerva herself. She has grown to be something of a sloven. It turns out that this seeking the kingdom of God by way of violence and revolt of the soul has had no other result than to debauch reason. The great existential existentialism, once it had been absorbed into the body of its enemy, succeeded only in bringing about, in philosophy itself, a philosophical destruction of the intellect, which is likely to yield profits for some years: a philosophical art of ideological proliferations of the absurd, cleverly barricaded behind Freudian analyses and phenomenological parentheses, and a complete philosophical liquidation of the basic realities and radical claims of the person and subjectivity.

Everything that was essentially linked with the supreme combat for the salvation of the self, or the imprecatory tension and posture of faith, has inevitably disappeared. The soul has been evacuated. The cry sent up to God, the frenzy or the despair born of excess of hope, the expectancy of miracle, the sense of sacrifice and the sense of sin, the spiritual agony, the eternal dignity of the existent, the grandeur of its liberty raised up on the ruins of its nature, all have necessarily been evacuated. Job has been evacuated: only the dunghill has been kept. The nothingness *in* the existent has been replaced by the nothingness *of* the existent. The horror of free nihilation which plunders existence has been replaced by the taking note of that natural non-being which *limitation* is in regard to existence, and with which the antinomies of the sovereign dialectic afflict the latter. Or it has been replaced by the experience of the threat with which the casual anybody holds over the *I;* or by the acceptance (in which pride at least receives its due) of the impotence of the *for-it-self* to do anything except corrode and nullify existence; and of the nausea which comes over the mind at the sight of the stupid gratuitousness of the *in-itself* and the radical absurdity of existence.[4] The moral tragedy has been replaced by a sophisticated metaphysics.

Every philosophy has its merits. I do not deny the merits of the philosophies of which I speak, nor the elements of truth they have been able to lay hold of. However disappointingly they may do so, their mere invocation of the words existence and liberty shows that they have at least been able to discern what was chiefly lacking in our contemporaries, and that

_____

[4] 'Thus, nothingness is that hole in being, that drop of the *in-itself* towards the self by which the *for-itself* is constituted.' J. P. Sartre, *L'Etre et le Néant,* p. 121. 'The *for-itself* therefore corresponds to a disrestraining destructuration of the *in-itself,* and the *in-itself* nullifies itself and is absorbed into its attempt to found itself. It is therefore not a substance of which the *for-itself* could be the attribute and which could produce thought without being absorbed into that production itself. It remains simply in the *for-itself* as a memory of being, as its unjustifiable *presence in the world. Being-in-itself* can found its nothingness, but not its being. In its decomposition it nullifies itself in a *for-itself* which becomes, as *for-itself,* its own basis. But its contingence as *in-itself* remains unassailable.' *Ibid.,* p. 127.

they are at least trying to make up, in their own way, for that which the systems of our great architects had most decidedly forgotten. My aim has been merely to indicate by what curve of a tolerably reliable logic, modern thought has moved from existential existentialism to academic existentialism, from the existentialism of faith to the atheistic existentialism.

I am aware that there are other forms of philosophical existentialism, and that there is, in particular, a Christian existentialism which challenges atheistic existentialism with a perspicacity all the keener and a pugnacity all the more lively for the fact that theirs is a family quarrel. In the order of a genuine phenomenology (where moral and psychological analysis is really an approach to ontological problems and where the very purity of an unprejudiced investigation allows philosophy to plumb human experience and to isolate its real meanings and values) this Christian existentialism is past master, and it contributes very valuable discoveries. Nevertheless, I do not believe that it can ever develop into a metaphysic properly so called, any more than any other philosophy which refuses to admit the intellectual intuition of being. It cannot father a metaphysics that is comprehensive, articulated, founded upon reason, and capable of exercising the functions of wisdom as well as of knowledge. For the same reason I do not believe that in the evolution of philosophical thought, it will ever succeed in becoming more than a side issue, nor will it successfully resist the historic impetus which at the present time gives to atheistic existentialism (and will in the future give to new systems issuing in like fashion out of the central positions of the long tradition that goes back to Descartes) an ephemeral but vast power over men's minds. To arrest that trend the springs would have to be purified all the way back to their original source. It would be necessary to overcome acquired habits and critical negligence accumulated in the course of three centuries, and to break with the errors common to existentialist irrationalism, idealism, empirical nominalism, and classical rationalism.

The Situation of Existentialism

34. 'We believe that the central intuition on which the existentialism of a Kierkegaard lived was in the last analysis the same as that which lies at the heart of Thomism. We refer to the intuition of the absolutely singular value and the primacy of the act of existing, the *existentia ut exercita*. But in Kierkegaard it sprang from the depths of a faith filled with anguish, robbed of its intelligible or superintelligible structure, desperately expecting the miraculous and rejecting the mystical possession for which it thirsts; it sprang from a radically irrationalist thought which rejects and sacrifices essences and falls back upon the night of subjectivity.'[5] These lines which I wrote elsewhere seem to me still to be true. But if it is correct to say that Kierkegaard's thought and attitude are, essentially and above all, religious, it is probably still more true to say that what Kierkegaard's existentialism lived on was something more than the intuition of the primacy of the act of existing. But on what? The word intuition is no longer appropriate

[5] Jacques Maritain, 'Coopération philosophique et Justice intellectuelle,' in *Revue Thomiste*, September-December, 1946 (*Raison et Raisons*, Chap. IV).

here. Let us say, rather, the dominating, devastating, absolute sense of the mystery of the infinite transcendence (attested by the Patriarchs and Prophets) of Him whose Name it is impossible to pronounce, placed above 'every name that is named, not only in this world, but also in that which is to come';[6] let us say the ever frustrated, yet ever more piercing thirst, the expectation (for to-day, for this miserable existent) of that destruction of sin and of death; that deliverance from slavery under the Law and under the necessities of the created world; that humiliation of 'that which is' and that choice of 'that which is not';[7] and that overwhelming liberty of which the Gospels brought us tidings.

All this, in fact, has reference to an attitude towards life rather than to doctrinal pronouncement. This meaning of the transcendence of the absolute and this expectancy of deliverance are the vital principle in the *imprecatory* attitude, in the attitude of dramatic singularity of which I spoke earlier in connection with Kierkegaard and Chestov. I by no means maintain that their doctrine was more faithful to the Old and New Testaments than that of other thinkers, both Jewish and Christian. Far from it! There was in them a kind of sublime aberration fatal to doctrine, and their fault, pregnant with consequences, was to believe that in order to glorify transcendence it was necessary to destroy reason; whereas what is necessary is to humiliate reason before the author of reason and by this act save it. Even if the initial fault lay with Hegel, who declared

___

[6] Ephesians I, 21. cf. Gen. XXXII, 29.

[7] Cf. I Corinthians I, 28: "Et ignobilia mundi, et contemptibilia elegit Deus, et ea, quae non sunt, ut ea quae sunt destrueret."

that philosophy—his philosophy—was the 'Science of Good and Evil' finally achieved, Chestov cannot be forgiven for identifying reason with the Serpent. Yet I think that Kierkegaard and Chestov felt more than other men, and to the bottom of their souls, that kind of shock or rending which leaves man no rest and no pity, and which (while it is certainly not to be confused with faith in the Gospels, and is sometimes, as with Chestov, a mere desire for that faith) is nevertheless the result of the nostalgic yearning infused by the Gospels in the veins of mankind. Short of the divine virtues there is nothing in man which better attests his grandeur than this trepidation. It is not by this means that philosophy accomplishes its work. Frenzy is allowable in the prophet. It is forbidden to the philosopher.

Neither Kierkegaard nor Chestov was able to do justice to the mystics. They cruelly and rather shabbily misunderstood them. Yet the experience and the 'nights' of the mystics was what they aspired to without being aware of it. If we try to situate them in their rightful place in the realm of the spirit, we must turn our eyes not towards philosophy but towards that apophatic contemplation in which God is known as unknown, in the perspective of which their efforts and their struggle derive their most genuine significance. They found obstacles in their path which they were unable to surmount. That path was the path of spiritual heroism. At its end they would have met their true companions. The place towards which they journeyed through the shadows was that place where souls possessed and illuminated by the madness of the Cross give their testimony.

If, now, we examine the other existentialism, philosophical or academic existentialism, in its most

typical forms, and in particular, atheistic existentialism, we shall see that it has rejected everything that
gave life to the 'first existential generation.' What
does this academic existentialism live on? What in
it constitutes that central intuition without which
there is no philosophy that is worth an hour's trou-
ble? Being philosophical or academic, and therefore
artful and cunning, it is not surprising that it should
conceal and dissemble that intuition, and take all
sorts of means to defend itself against it. Herr
Heidegger, who is not lacking in the gift of oppor-
tunism, recently went so far as to repudiate the word
existentialism. And in the first chapter of this brief
treatise I pointed out the zeal with which atheistic
existentialism bestirs itself to render man's condition
of 'useless passion' a source of comfort to him. It remains that behind the diverse strongholds which
each particular system builds for itself, the central
intuition at work in the existentialism in question is
the perfectly simple and perfectly enlightening one
of the *nihil* whence we come and towards which we
tend ('All that comes from nothing,' St. Thomas
wrote, 'tends of itself towards nothing'[8])—the intuition of pure nothingness (which is the sole residue
discoverable in the creature once the Creative Action has been suppressed) and of the radical absurdity of an existence uprooted from God.

Atheistic existentialism is a philosophy, it has a
real experience of liberty, though cloudy and disap-
pointing. But spiritual experience and transcendent
apperceptions do not seem to be its strong side. Even
in the prolongations furnished it by literature and
the artistic imagination its discoveries in that order

[8] *De Veritate*, V, 2.

have not the depth of those of, say, Marcel Jouhan-
deau's novels and tales. At the same time, it is round
a certain spiritual experience that this whole philosophy proliferates. If we look for the place where its
most genuine significance may be made apparent in
the realm of the spirit, we must say, I believe, that
the by no means negligible position which it occupies in that realm is that of a highly elaborate metaphysic of the condition in which man finds himself
when he willingly espouses the nothingness out of
which he came, when he becomes a witness within
himself to the disagregation of being by nothingness,
and deliberately chooses misery because he prefers
it to not being the first (nihilating) cause in the exercise of his liberty. Just as there are, here below,
anticipations of eternal life (which do not necessarily involve a destiny) so there are anticipations of
hell. The latter play no indifferent part in the life
of man, and particularly modern man. We are bound
to acknowledge the interesting character of a philosophy which, even when it strives by every means
to conceal from itself its own meaning, scrutinises
man's condition and reconstructs the problem of being in the perspective of those anticipations. Such a
philosophy hollows out a void from which a genuine
metaphysic of being may perhaps have some chance
of coming forth.

Having made up its mind to be the sole supreme
knowledge and so to replace theology, philosophy
has for three centuries assumed the heritage and the
burdens of theology. The great modern metaphysical
systems are thus only seemingly liberated from theology. The questions which the latter claimed to answer continue to haunt those systems. Nowhere is
this plainer than in the philosophy of Hegel. It is

not useless to remark that atheistic existentialism itself remains dependent upon theology, though an inverted theology. For it, as for Marxism, atheism is a
point of departure accepted in advance. These two
antagonistic philosophies, the one rationalist, the
other irrationalist, both develop in the light of an
a-theo-logy of which they are the *ancillae*. From this
it follows that all the avenues of being are closed to
them, because they are too liable to lead in the direction of the transcendent Being. However great
their hostility to idealism, those philosophies *cannot*
set themselves up as philosophies of being. Moreover, the very name of existentialism is, as regards
atheistic existentialism, a name usurped. Neither being nor existence: such philosophies are in reality
philosophies of action, either of *praxis* and the trans-
forming action of the world, or of moral creation *a
nihilo* and liberty for liberty's sake. This is why the
very notion of contemplation has become unthinkable for them, and they have no other resource than,
in the fine scorn of ignorance, to stigmatise with the
name of 'quietism' the highest and purest activity of
the intellect, the free activity of fruition of truth.

The Autonomy of Philosophy

35. St. Thomas distinguished in order to unite,
wherefore he distinguished only the more clearly
and powerfully. At a moment in the history of cul-
ture when Christian thought, dominated by the Au-
gustinian tradition, felt loth to make way for purely
rational disciplines, one of the principal objects of
his work was to distinguish philosophy from theology
in an irrefutable fashion and thus to establish the

autonomy of philosophy. He did succeed in establishing this autonomy in principle. After him, that
autonomy was never truly established in fact and is
not yet so established. The nominalism of the Scho-
lastics who came after St. Thomas could not but
jeopardise that autonomy when they dispossessed
metaphysics of its certitudes and allotted them ex-
clusively to the supra-rational domain of faith. The
philosophical imperialism of the great thinkers who
came after Descartes jeopardised it in another and
contrary fashion by dispossessing theological wisdom
in order to burden metaphysics and moral philosophy, as I said a moment ago, with the major offices
and supreme responsibilities which theology had
had in its keeping. Philosophy thereafter took these
offices and responsibilities upon itself, at first with
vainglorious optimism but afterwards with the black
pessimism of all great disillusions. The system of
Malebranche is a theophilosophy. The monadism of
Leibnitz is a metaphysical transposition of the treatise on the Angels. The morality of Kant is a philosophical transposition of the Decalogue. The positivism of Auguste Comte opened out into the religion
of Humanity. The panlogism of Hegel was the supreme effort of modern philosophy to absorb all the
realms of the spirit into the absolutism of reason.
After that came the despair of reason, but it was a
reason still held, still wounded by the theological obsession which had now become an anti-theological
obsession. When Feuerbach declared that God was
the creation and the alienation of man; when Nietzsche proclaimed the death of God, they were the
theologians of our contemporary atheistic philosophies. Why are these philosophies so charged with
bitterness, unless it is because they feel themselves

chained in spite of themselves to a transcendence and to a past they constantly have to kill, and in the negation of which their own roots are planted?

There is thus a curious analogy between the situation of our own age and that of the XIIIth Century. If philosophy is to be freed from the deformities resulting from an enduring servitude, either to the theological heritage in the Christian régime or to the anti-theological heritage in the atheistic régime; if it is to win its autonomy—not only in principle but in fact—it will still owe this boon to Aristotle and Thomas Aquinas. Meanwhile, one should stress the conditional character of this proposition. For up to now—as far as Christian thought is concerned—neither in metaphysics nor (particularly) in ethics have the Thomists been very zealous in their effort fully to disengage the proper structure of their philosophy from the methods of approach and the problematics of their theology. Too often their philosophy makes its appearance as the transposition into the field of reason of a theology deprived of its own light which is faith, without, moreover, having carried on the work of reorganisation and recasting which would have given to the *opus philosophicum* the structural constitution and intrinsic order proper to philosophy. An authentically philosophical soul thus animates a body which it has not completely shaped and moulded and which is not expressly proportioned to it. Besides, we have no reassurance that the theologians of our own age will not commit the same mistake as their ancestors of the XIVth Century. Will they not prefer perhaps to try for a time to keep their hold on men's minds, and maintain a kind of theological imperialism, rather than put the weapons and wholesome distinctions of St. Thomas to work? Will they not try perhaps to incorporate into theology itself and utilise for theological ends any themes whatever of the philosophy of their time (sweetened and watered down, of course, and adapted to the requirements of faith) rather than leave to a philosophy genuinely equipped with St. Thomas's principles the leisure to develop in its autonomous field, leave to it, also, the task of rescuing from the modern systems the truths from which the latter draw their momentary strength?

We are still less assured, in another connection, that the philosophers—yesterday rationalistic, to-day atheistic—who carry on the modern tradition, will be capable of being regenerated in the primordial intuitions of reason and the articulated disciplines of a philosophy unquestionably liberated from the chains of all pseudo-theology and anti-theology.

For in fact—and here is where the shoe pinches— the order and laws of the things of the spirit are inviolable. Philosophy will never truly free itself from all deforming servitude to the theological or the anti-theological heritage, will never be truly autonomous, unless it recognise the existence and value proper to theology, and thereby preserve its own autonomy (which is not supreme) by the free and normal avowal of its infravalence in comparison with the wisdoms that are higher than it. St. Thomas established philosophy in its own domain. He distinguished it from theology with a clarity and a firmness that cannot be broken. But he did so only by ensuring cohesion in difference and by affirming the intrinsic superiority of theological wisdom over metaphysical wisdom, and of mystical wisdom over theological wisdom. There is nothing to be done about this order, because it does not depend upon us. Only on the condition that we respect it can we preserve, at every degree, the autonomy of each and all the forms of knowing.

Yet these considerations, which concern essences or quiddities, are still not sufficient. The conditions or requirements of the existential order must also be taken into account. Thomist principles not only carry distinction and unity into the ordering of knowledge. They also disclose the quickening and strengthening which each degree receives from the others in the existential context and concrete reality of the life of the spirit. They oblige us to realise how, at the immaterial node of the soul's energies, mystical wisdom and theological wisdom vivify and fortify metaphysical wisdom just as the latter itself vivifies and fortifies philosophical activities of a lower rank.[9]

Here arises the question hotly debated a few years ago concerning what we must call Christian philosophy although that name is ambiguous. It may be described as Christian, not on account of its essence, indeed, but only on account of its state or conditions of existence. This is the case in the domain of speculative philosophy. Or it may be described as Christian on account of the use which it makes, within its very texture, of truths of another order established in theology by reason of the existential state of its very subject (human conduct). This is the case in the domain of moral philosophy. I have discussed elsewhere this question of Christian philosophy[10] and shall confine myself here to remarking that St.

[9] Cf. *Science et Sagesse*, ch. III and 'Elucidations.' Eng. trans., pp. 70-136, 228-362.

[10] Cf. J. Maritain, *De la philosophie chrétienne* and *Science et Sagesse*.

Thomas, without explicitly dealing with it, took an extremely clear position on it. He affirmed this position not only by his principles but by his action,— by fighting and suffering; for his whole battle was to gain recognition for Aristotle and to overthrow Averroës, which is to say, to gain recognition of the essential autonomy of philosophy and at the same time to link it vitally, in its human exercise, with the higher illumination of theological wisdom and the wisdom of the saints. 'If today there are Thomist writers who are shocked by the very idea of a Christian philosophy, this simply proves that one can repeat a master's formula without knowing of what spirit one is, and that Thomism, like every other great doctrine, can be dissected like a corpse by professors of anatomy instead of being thought by philosophers.'[11]

Philosophy and Spiritual Experience

36. Whatever the subject dealt with in the preceding pages, whether it was the primacy of the *act of existing* in metaphysics and in the theory of knowledge; or, in moral philosophy, the fundamentally existential character of the judgment of conscience and the judgment of prudence and the existential finalities of moral philosophy itself; or the central importance accorded to the existent and the subject in the universe of being; or the theory of evil and the part attributable to the free existent and to the frailties of his liberty in the perspectives which Thomist principles open to us upon the eternal

[11] Cf. *De Bergson à Thomas d'Aquin,* p. 317.

purposes—we have seen how the existentialism of Thomas Aquinas differs from modern existentialism, both because it is rational in type and because, being founded upon the intuitiveness of the senses and the intellect, it associates and identifies being and intelligibility at every point. Descartes and the whole rationalist philosophy born of the Cartesian revolution raised a wall of insuperable enmity between intellect and mystery, and this is doubtless the deepest source of the fundamental inhumanity of every civilisation based upon rationalism. St. Thomas reconciles intellect and mystery at the core of being, at the core of existence. He thereby liberates our intellect, restores it to its nature by restoring it to its object. Thereby, also, he makes it possible for us to effect unity within ourselves, and, without having to repudiate reason and philosophy, to win liberty and peace, though in regions which transcend philosophy and which are not to be reached by any path of philosophy.

We are here in the presence of the most significant privilege of that great zeal for being which animates Thomist thought and renders it so desperately necessary while at the same time so foreign and intolerable to the emptied, exasperated, ailing reason of our time. Thomist thought is a creator of unity; we cherish dispersion. It is a creator of liberty; we go in quest of any sort of collective yoke. It is a creator of peace; and violence is our preference. The ills that rend us are what we love most in the world. We do not want to be set free.

And yet the great dumb ox out of Sicily began to bellow through the world very long ago, and he is not going to stop as soon as all that. It is open to every man, if he so choose, to listen to him. If his spirit and his doctrine tend to create unity in man it is always by virtue of the same secret—which is to understand all things in the light and the generosity of being. Nature and grace, faith and reason, theology and philosophy, the supernatural virtues and the natural virtues, wisdom and science, speculative energies and the practical energies, the world of metaphysics and the world of ethics, the world of knowledge and of poetry and of mystical silence—St. Thomas scrupulously recognises the domain and the rights appertaining to each of these constellations in the human heavens; but he does not tear them asunder. In his existential perspective he establishes upon diversity a unity which is that of the Image of God, and he causes all our powers to converge in a synergy which saves and stimulates our whole being.[12] He is at the opposite pole from Hegel, who disunited all things and sowed war among them by placing the universality of being in the anti-existentialist perspective of an absolute idealism, and by endeavouring to subject all things to the unity of the great cosmogonical Idol in which contradictories are coupled for monstrous begettings, and where Being and Nothingness are made one.

37. We should be grateful to Kierkegaard and his successors for having, in their fight against Hegel, taught anew, to those who profess to be thinkers, the great lesson of anguish; and in particular for having reminded the disciples of St. Thomas of that great lesson. The mortal danger run by those whose doctrine mounts towards the heights of unity and peace is that they may think they have reached their

---

[12] Cf. *De Bergson à Thomas d'Aquin*, p. 316.

goal when they have only started on the path, and
that they may forget that for man and his thought,
peace is always a victory over discord, and unity the
reward of wrenchings suffered and conquered.

Thomist peace and unity bear no relation to the
facile balancings and the dialectical conciliations
practiced by a reason installed in the security of an
apparatus of ready-made answers that come forth at
the click of every imaginable question. They call for
never-ending triumphs over ceaselessly recurring
conflicts. They require involvement in the thick of
new questions in order to bring forth a fresh intuition
of new truths, or cause old truths newly penetrated
to gush forth from the rock of acquired knowing.
They demand communion with all the strivings of
research and discovery to release into the light that
truth which those strivings ordinarily attain only
with the help of the ferments of error, or in ill-fated
conceptualisations. They exact from man a tension
and an extension which, in truth, are possible only
in the anguish of the Cross. For what St. Paul said
is true also in the order of the things of the spirit:
there is no redemption without the shedding of
blood. The reconciliation of the supreme energies of
intelligence and of life which, like every appetite
for the absolute, are naturally ferocious, each claiming everything for itself, is a false reconciliation if
it is not also a redemption; and it cannot be accomplished except at the price of an ordeal of suffering
of which the spirit itself is the locus.[13]

As a philosophical category, anguish is worthless.
It is not the stuff out of which a philosophy is made
any more than it is the stuff they make divers' suits

[13] Cf. *De Bergson à Thomas d'Aquin,* pp. 133-134.

out of. It happens that anguish is found inside a diver's suit, but it does not enter into its composition. Anguish is the lot of subjectivity. It is in the philosopher, not in his philosophy. If it passes into his philosophy, the reason is that his philosophy has been infected by his ego, and also because his ego has found this means of soothing itself. To excogitate anguish is more comfortable than to suffer it.

Where is there a philosopher for whom anguish is not the companion of his destiny? To beat our heads against the wall when the *why?* escapes us is nothing extraordinary. The longing for death always comes when the work of pouring truths into the mould of our truest words seems to be treason to truth. Happy are they whose anguish has been transfigured by the purity of tears. The biographers of St. Thomas tell us that he wept much: the masterpiece of serenest objectivity was born in the tears of a saint. St. Thomas did not work in peace but in conflict and in haste (and what are we all but men condemned to die, hastening strangely to pronounce our message before passing on to the place where all messages are useless and where all things are visible in their nakedness?). He was so anxious to know, that he pressed his brow against the altar to find the light, and disturbed Peter and Paul to obtain from them enlightenment on his doubts. For he was responsible for the heaviest of tasks: he had to carry, to orientate, to realign without losing the least scrap of it, the whole universe of Christian thought for the time to come; and the least fault would have meant the ruin of everything. Meanwhile there were his attentive colleagues, who spied upon his every move and sought every occasion to tumble his work into some ditch of the cemetery of heresies—and did in fact succeed in having his doctrine condemned at Paris and at Oxford when he was no longer there to defend it. Was this why he wept? He wept as he gazed at the mystery of being; he wept because he saw enough to faint under the flood of that which he did not see.

This is a thing very far beyond anguish. Anguish is no more than one form of the spiritual experience of the philosopher. In proportion as he goes forward, the philosopher moves through other states: he knows the intellectual joy (into which nothing human penetrates) of decisive intuitions and illuminating certainties—a sort of intoxication with the object which is almost cruel—and sometimes the freezing exaltation of the glance that denudes and destroys; and sometimes the revulsion of handling those animal skeletons and bones of the dead of which Goethe speaks; and sometimes the ardour which wounds him on every side for the infinite search which men carry on and for all captive truths; sometimes the pity for error with its ambiguities; and sometimes the great solitude or distress of the spirit; and sometimes the sweetness of going forward in the maternal night. What I should like to stress is that the spiritual experience of the philosopher is the nourishing soil of philosophy; that without it there is no philosophy; and that, even so, spiritual experience does not, or must not, enter into the intelligible texture of philosophy. The pulp of the fruit must consist of nothing but the truth.

And now, if it is true that philosophy tends to go beyond itself in order to attain to the silence of unity, where it will harvest all that it knows in a purer and more transparent light, what is the experience in which it (whose first object is the world and man) can cause the spirit of man thus to expand, unless it be the experience of the gift of knowledge? Then will man attain peace, then will he be able to say, *ecce in pace amaritudo mea amarissima.* What the gift of knowledge produces, according to John of St. Thomas,[14] is a certain experience or a *taste* of creatures which detaches us from them, a spiritual experience of created being which induces in us a yearning for God. 'Thou art the Lord our God. In very deed the hills were liars, and the multitude of the mountains. Behold, we come to thee . . .'[15] To what truer knowledge can the philosopher lay claim? He will have received his due when, one day, not by the discourse of reason but by a simple and intimate experience—in which all seems said, and in which compassion is made one with detachment—he will know that beings, with all their beauty, differ from the infinite Being more than they resemble Him. When he will know how great is the abandonment of those who, to hold the created being within reach, were forced to scale the glaciers of the void where they see everywhere the void. When he will know that there is nothing more despised and rejected among men than the truth he loves, and will feel that for that truth every opportunity is a lost opportunity, and that its highest messages, if they are purely human, influence history only as a nudge to the blind and only when they can no longer be deciphered. When he will discern the irrefutable meaning of the *mihi videtur ut palea* and perceive that all that men have said about being and God must seem to the saints like a bundle of straw, and

---

[14] Jean de St. Thomas, *Les Dons du Saint-Esprit,* translated by Raïssa Maritain, Paris, 1930, pp. 169-179.

[15] Jeremiah III, 22-23.

that the wisp which each man strives with so much labour to add to the bundle will not serve him, for it is according to his love that he will be judged. When he will understand that all the treasures of the intelligibility of being, all the glory of the *act of existing*, and the savour of the existent which he so much wished to taste, have always regarded him with infinite indifference and never wished to give themselves to him. For it was he who, by the law of the human intellect focussing its light upon the booty of the senses, had sought to seize those treasures by piercing the veil for a single instant. Therefore from the beginning he accepted disappointment, for we incur inevitable disappointment when we seek to take that which refuses to give itself. The hills may have been liars, but it was not the hills that disappointed him. One day the hills will surrender themselves, everything will surrender itself to the intelligence of man on the day when the self-subsistent *Act of Existing* shall give Itself in vision.

Rome, January-April, 1947.

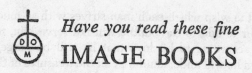

Have you read these fine
IMAGE BOOKS

OUR LADY OF FATIMA
By William Thomas Walsh

The strange and beautiful story of the miraculous appearance of the Blessed Virgin before three humble shepherd children, and its world-wide significance.

D1—65c

DAMIEN THE LEPER
By John Farrow

A story of courage, devotion and sacrifice that has become a living legend throughout the world.

D3—65c

A POPULAR HISTORY OF THE CATHOLIC CHURCH
By Philip Hughes

A complete one-volume history of the Church from its earliest days down to the contemporary scene.

D4—85c

PEACE OF SOUL
By Fulton J. Sheen

A brilliant, significant message of inspiration for those troubled souls seeking peace in the turbulent modern atomic age. By one of the world's outstanding religious leaders.

D8—75c

THE SPIRIT OF CATHOLICISM
By Karl Adam

A brilliant exposition of Catholicism and an explanation of the true spirit of the Catholic Church.

D2—75c

MR. BLUE
By Myles Connolly

A modern classic about a contemporary St. Francis that will make you pause and wonder about your own way of life.

D5—50c

THE DIARY OF A COUNTRY PRIEST
By Georges Bernanos

A compassionate novel of French village life that reflects the spiritual conflicts and struggles of all mankind.

D6—65c

THE CHURCH SPEAKS TO THE MODERN WORLD:
The Social Teachings of Leo XIII
Edited by Etienne Gilson

The great encyclicals of Pope Leo XIII, arranged as he directed, presenting his social order. Introduction and notes by the distinguished philosopher, Etienne Gilson.

D7—95c

If your bookseller is unable to supply certain titles, write to Image Books, Department MIB, Garden City, New York, stating the titles you desire and enclosing the price of each book (plus 5¢ per book to cover cost of postage and handling). Prices are subject to change without notice.

Image Books

*. . . making the world's finest
Catholic literature available to all*

Image Books

THE IMITATION OF CHRIST
by Thomas à Kempis, edited with an Introduction by Harold C. Gardiner, S.J.
A modern version, based on the Whitford translation, of the immortal spiritual classic.
D17—65¢

THE EVERLASTING MAN
by G. K. Chesterton
The great classic of G. K. Chesterton in which he brilliantly and wittily proves that Christianity is the only true religion.
D18—75¢

A GRAMMAR OF ASSENT
by John Henry Newman with an Introduction by Etienne Gilson
One of the most significant works of the great English Cardinal in which the problem of assent to religious truths is discussed.
D19—95¢

A WATCH IN THE NIGHT
by Helen C. White
A magnificent novel in which the full and varied life of the Middle Ages is vividly portrayed.
D20—95¢

BROTHER PETROC'S RETURN
by S. M. C.
A delightful story of a monk buried in the 16th century who comes to life in the 20th century.
D21—50¢

ST. FRANCIS OF ASSISI
by Johannes Jörgensen
The definitive biography of the most beloved of all saints.
D22—95¢

STORIES OF OUR CENTURY BY CATHOLIC AUTHORS
edited by John Gilland Brunini and Francis X. Connolly
Twenty-five of the best short stories of the 20th century by the outstanding authors of our times.
D23—85¢

AUTOBIOGRAPHY OF A HUNTED PRIEST
by John Gerard with an Introduction by Graham Greene
The moving and exciting story of a Jesuit priest in Elizabethan England.
D24—85¢

FATHER MALACHY'S MIRACLE
by Bruce Marshall
A witty, sparkling novel of a humble Scottish priest who proves to all unbelievers and skeptics that the age of miracles is not past.
D25—65¢

ON THE TRUTH OF THE CATHOLIC FAITH (SUMMA CONTRA GENTILES) Book One: God
by St. Thomas Aquinas, newly translated, with an Introduction and notes by Anton C. Pegis
A superb new translation of St. Thomas Aquinas' classic statement of the enduring truths of Christianity.
D26—85¢

Image Books

. . . making the world's finest
Catholic literature available to all

THE WORLD'S FIRST LOVE
by Fulton J. Sheen
The whole story of Mary, Mother of God, lovingly and reverently portrayed in the inimitable style of the great Bishop.   D30—75¢

THE SIGN OF JONAS
by Thomas Merton
The absorbing day-by-day account of life in a Trappist monastery by one of the great spiritual writers of our times.
D31—95¢

PARENTS, CHILDREN AND THE FACTS OF LIFE
by Henry V. Sattler, C.SS.R.
An invaluable guide for parents and teachers for sex instruction of children, based on tested and approved Catholic methods and principles.
D32—65¢

LIGHT ON THE MOUNTAIN
The Story of LaSalette
by John S. Kennedy
The miraculous appearance of the Blessed Virgin Mary at LaSalette in 1846 dramatically and inspiringly portrayed.
D33—65¢

EDMUND CAMPION
by Evelyn Waugh
The heroic life of the great English Jesuit and martyr told in the matchless prose of one of England's greatest authors.
D34—65¢

HUMBLE POWERS
by Paul Horgan
Three beautifully told novelettes which magnificently emphasize the eternal power of faith, love and sacrifice.
D35—65¢

SAINT THOMAS AQUINAS
by G. K. Chesterton
A superb introduction to the work and personality of the Angelic Doctor by the scintillating and irresistible G.K.C.
D36—75¢

ON THE TRUTH OF THE CATHOLIC FAITH (SUMMA CONTRA GENTILES) BOOK TWO: CREATION
by St. Thomas Aquinas, newly translated, with an Introduction and notes, by James F. Anderson.
The second volume of the new translation of St. Thomas Aquinas' great classic *Summa Contra Gentiles.*   D27—95¢

If your bookseller is unable to supply certain titles, write to Image Books, Department MIB, Garden City, New York, stating the titles you desire and enclosing the price of each book (plus 5¢ per book to cover cost of postage and handling). Prices are subject to change without notice.

Image Books

. . . making the world's finest
Catholic literature available to all

APOLOGIA PRO VITA SUA
by John Henry Newman
Introduction by Philip Hughes
Definitive edition of the great
English cardinal's superb spiritual autobiography. D37—95¢

A HANDBOOK OF THE CATHOLIC FAITH
by Dr. N. G. M. Van Doornik,
Rev. S. Jelsma, Rev. A. Van De
Lisdonk. Edited by Rev. John
Greenwood.
A complete summary of every
aspect of Catholic doctrine and
practice. 520 pp. D38—$1.35

THE NEW TESTAMENT
Official Catholic edition
Newly translated into English
by members of the Catholic
Biblical Association of America
under the supervision of the
Episcopal Committee of the
Archconfraternity of Christian
Doctrine. D39—95¢

ON THE TRUTH OF THE CATHOLIC FAITH (SUMMA CONTRA GENTILES) Book Three: *Providence,* Part I
by St. Thomas Aquinas, newly
translated, with an Introduction
and notes, by Vernon J. Bourke
The third book of the new
translation of St. Thomas' magnificent classic *Summa Contra
Gentiles.* Part 1 contains chapters 1 to 83. D28A—85¢

MARIA CHAPDELAINE
by Louis Hémon
A novel of French-Canadian
life which has justly been called
an idyllic epic. D40—65¢

SAINT AMONG THE HURONS
by Francis X. Talbot, S.J.
The stirring and inspiring story
of Jean de Brébeuf, one of the
American martyrs, who was
tortured and put to death by
the Indians. D41—95¢

THE PATH TO ROME
by Hilaire Belloc
The delightful account of a
most unusual pilgrimage on foot
to Rome. Illustrated by the
author. D42—85¢

SORROW BUILT A BRIDGE
by Katherine Burton
The biography of Nathaniel
Hawthorne's daughter—her conversion to Catholicism and her
work as Mother Alphonsa,
founder of a religious order.
D43—75¢

ON THE TRUTH OF THE CATHOLIC FAITH (SUMMA CONTRA GENTILES) Book Three: *Providence,* Part 2
by St. Thomas Aquinas, newly
translated, with an Introduction
and notes, by Vernon J. Bourke
Part 2 contains chapters 84 to
163. D28B—85¢

If your bookseller is unable to supply certain titles, write to Image
Books, Department MIB, Garden City, New York, stating the titles
you desire and enclosing the price of each book (plus 5¢ per book
to cover cost of postage and handling). Prices are subject to change
without notice.

Image Books

*. . . making the world's finest
Catholic literature available to all*

THE WISE MAN FROM THE WEST
by Vincent Cronin

Vivid, fascinating account of a remarkable priest who brought Christianity to the strange world of sixteenth century China.
D44—85¢

EXISTENCE AND THE EXISTENT
by Jacques Maritain

Existentialism, the most discussed trend in modern philosophy, examined in the light of Thomist thought by a world-famed Catholic philosopher.
D45—75¢

THE STORY OF THE TRAPP FAMILY SINGERS
by Maria Augusta Trapp

The delightful story of a remarkable family. "Engrossing, humorous, poignant," says Boston Traveler.
D46—85¢

THE WORLD, THE FLESH AND FATHER SMITH
by Bruce Marshall

The heartwarming story of a lovable priest. "Delightfully written," said the New York Times of this wise and witty book.
D47—65¢

THE CHRIST OF CATHOLICISM
by Dom Aelred Graham

A full, well-rounded study of Christ, His personality and teaching, by the distinguished Benedictine writer.
D48—95¢

ST. FRANCIS XAVIER
by James Brodrick, S.J.

A new condensed version for modern readers of the biography of St. Francis that the New York Times calls: "the best book on Francis Xavier in any language."
D49—95¢

ST. FRANCIS OF ASSISI
by G. K. Chesterton

A fresh, fascinating study of one of the best-loved saints—by one of the outstanding writers of our time.
D50—65¢

ON THE TRUTH OF THE CATHOLIC FAITH (SUMMA CONTRA GENTILES) BOOK FOUR: SALVATION
by St. Thomas Aquinas. Translated, with an Introduction and notes, by Charles J. O'Neil

The final volume of the superb new English translation of this great Christian classic.
D29—95¢

If your bookseller is unable to supply certain titles, write to Image Books, Department MIB, Garden City, New York, stating the titles you desire and enclosing the price of each book (plus 5¢ per book to cover cost of postage and handling). Prices are subject to change without notice.

IMAGE BOOKS

Image Books constitute a quality library of Catholic writings, broad in human interest and deep in Christian insight. They will include classical Christian writings, devotion, philosophy, education and history; biographies, novels and poetry; and books on contemporary social problems. They represent a planned program of making available to the widest possible audience the finest Catholic literature in attractive, paper-bound, inexpensive editions. They have been selected with these criteria in mind: that they must in every instance be well written, inspiring to the spirit, and of lasting value to the general audience who will purchase them.

The majority of Image Books will consist of reprints made possible through the cooperation of the publishers of the original editions. Occasionally certain much-needed volumes which are not available will also be initiated for this series.

A descriptive catalogue of the Image Books already published may be obtained by writing directly to the publisher. Comments and suggestions from those interested in the series are welcomed by the publisher.